Approaches to **Teaching** and **Learning**

Including Pupils with Learning Difficulties

Ron Babbage, Richard Byers
and Helen Redding

David Fulton Publishers
London

David Fulton Publishers Ltd
Ormond House, 26–27 Boswell Street, London WC1N 3JD

First published in Great Britain in 1999 by David Fulton Publishers
Reprinted 2000

Note: The right of Ron Babbage, Richard Byers and Helen Redding to be identified as the authors of this work has been asserted by them in accordance with the Copyright, Designs and Patents Act 1988.

Copyright © Ron Babbage, Richard Byers and Helen Redding 1999

British Library Cataloguing in Publication Data
A catalogue record for this book is available from the British Library

ISBN 1–85346–575–5

Typeset by Textype Typesetters, Cambridge
Printed in Great Britain by Bell and Bain Ltd, Glasgow.

Contents

Acknowledgements

We acknowledge the support of the following people:

Erica Brown, of the Centre for the Study of Special Education at Westminster College, Oxford, for providing us with the title of our project and for being a constant source of inspiration;

staff, governors, pupils and students at St John's School, Kempston and, in particular, Yvonne Cawdell, Veronica Pryke, Jacky Bingham and Anne Tredget, Barbara Doyle and Veronica Scargill;

staff and students at the University of Cambridge School of Education;

the Learning Support Team for the London Borough of Newham;

staff at The Walnuts School, Milton Keynes;

Claire Taylor for the hours she devoted to word processing our manuscript; our families and friends for being there and remaining there;

Mike and Robert Dewe for technical support;

David Fulton and colleagues at David Fulton Publishing for their support and for the award of the 1998/99 Fulton Fellowship;

without whom this publication would not have been possible.

Foreword

There is no doubt that inclusion will be the single most important educational issue at the beginning of the 21st century. National governments across the globe will, in the decades ahead, be seeking to make schools more inclusive. This may happen for the best of reasons – like the ideal of promoting an inclusive society in which there are equal opportunities for all. On the other hand, it may happen for less commendable reasons – it may simply be governments' reflex response to a legislative climate which is increasingly anti-discriminatory. But whatever the reasons, there is no doubt that inclusion will happen at an accelerating pace in the years ahead.

This presents some serious challenges for teachers, because schools in the 20th century have been segregative. Legislators and administrators have allowed curricula and pastoral systems to develop in mainstream schools as though 2 per cent of the population did not exist. As a result, schools are not now geared-up to educate 'special' children, and the reflex response to a child who presents serious challenges is usually an immediate search for special school placement.

Because populations of children have been separated in this way – into mainstream and special schools – it has meant that alternative curricula and teaching methods have been developed in special education for its 'special' populations. One would hope, given the money and time spent developing these, that they could have been demonstrated to do something useful. Unfortunately research shows the reverse to be the case. Although new teaching methods often are received in a fizz of excitement about their efficacy, more mature reflection and evaluation demonstrates that the new method is usually an elaborate waste of time – and may, indeed, do harm.

The message of all the research into the efficacy of teaching methods is that good teaching is good teaching, almost irrespective of the nature of the class: there are no magic cures. The corollary to this message is that inclusive environments can work as effectively as segregative ones – and this is another conclusion which is backed up by research. This is why this book from Ron Babbage, Richard Byers and Helen Redding is so exciting. It takes as a starting point the notion that it is *good teaching* which is important in the move to inclusion. It is good teaching which is vital – not the latest wonder-drug or the most fashionable, recently developed method of teaching.

It's exciting also because it is a book from practitioners, not putative experts delivering from on high. Despite exhortations from academics extolling the virtues of action research carried out by practitioners, there are precious few examples of such action research to be guided by. This book is exemplary in that it gives a detailed case study of research in action. It is a case study in reflective practice, and a fascinating one. Throughout, there is a resolute commitment to the notion that good practice in teaching is good practice for all children – never at any time do the authors succumb to the tempting illusion that special methods of assessment or weird and wonderful techniques will provide a 'cure' for children's problems at school.

In that sense, this is a truly mature book which has learned the lessons of research, and it is fitting that it should be published at the turn of a new century. It has taken us a great deal of time to learn the painful lesson that the search for special methods is hollow and that their 'discovery' is illusory. This book, unlike so many still being published, starts by providing an intelligent critique of existing theory and practice, out of which the authors adroitly synthesise some beautifully clear accounts of what characterises good teaching – for individuals or for groups – and it offers pointers about how school systems can be used to enable development in teaching. Perhaps most importantly, at the heart of the book is the implicit notion that education should be about what the Canadian educator Frank Smith calls 'the classical theory of learning' – the idea that learning is easy, as long as it is interesting and perceived to be relevant, and as long as teaching is sensitive to both the interests and the frailties of the learner. In the context of this classical theory, 'special educational needs' is something of a misnomer, since we all need the same things to learn, and this implicit understanding is central to what the authors are saying in this excellent book.

It is fitting also that it is the Fulton Fellowship which has enabled the book to be produced. David Fulton Publishers have, for over a decade, been producing a stream of publications which enable teachers to think about, change, and enhance their practice. Some of these books have provided good, practical guidance for the classroom, while others have been at the cutting edge of thinking about children who experience difficulty. The Fulton Fellowship has been David Fulton's way of 'putting back' into the educational community; it has certainly paid dividends with this book.

Gary Thomas
Chair in Education
Oxford Brookes University
July 1999

1 Introduction

What is the purpose of this book and who is it for?

It is clear that increased levels of interest in the prospect of including pupils with learning difficulties in schools and classrooms alongside their mainstream peers will be sustained in years to come. Much has now been written about the structures and school improvement procedures which might support this process of inclusion (for example, Clark *et al.* 1997; Thomas *et al.* 1998) and there is also a growing literature devoted to the development of an inclusive curriculum (see, for example, the *for All* series inaugurated by the MEC Teacher Fellows (1990) or Carpenter *et al.* 1996). As this debate proceeds, and a number of questions are resolved, the key issue of how to include pupils with learning difficulties within day to day classroom practice remains. We know this to be the case because we have talked at length with colleagues whose work involves supporting pupils with learning difficulties in more inclusive settings. These practitioners will often say that access for these learners – to new learning environments, to a wider and more diverse peer group, or to a broad and balanced curriculum – has been secured. They will also say that challenges remain in promoting full and meaningful participation. This issue often turns, in our experience, on pedagogy and on the extent to which there is a match between the teaching methods selected by staff, and pupils' innate or acquired learning preferences, skills and difficulties.

In the following pages we propose to focus, therefore, on the teaching and learning processes which will facilitate organisational and curricular inclusion for pupils with learning difficulties. Our purpose is to provide practical approaches, grounded in our understanding of theory, to the analysis of:

- the teaching methods used with pupils with learning difficulties;
- the learning preferences, strengths and areas of challenge of individual pupils with learning difficulties;
- the organisational, cultural and contextual factors which impinge upon the development of more inclusive educational provision.

This is not a book which is simply about relocation. We suggest that the issues we address will be relevant whether staff are seeking to include pupils with learning difficulties within mainstream classes or pupils with severe and complex or profound and multiple learning difficulties within teaching groups with their age peers in specialist contexts. We propose that all schools and all classrooms can be part of the project of making teaching and learning more inclusive. We would also argue, with Ainscow (1991), that what is needed to drive this project forward 'is for each teacher to seek deeper understandings of the nature and outcomes of particular educational events and situations'. While the origins and potential outcomes of this project therefore lie in practice, improvements in the quality of teaching and learning for pupils with learning difficulties will mean improvements in teaching and learning for all and, ultimately, whole school improvement, as Ainscow makes clear.

We wrote this book with a clear sense of audience. We assume that it might be read and put to practical use by:

- anyone interested in the education of pupils with learning difficulties, including teachers, classroom co-educators, parents and carers and other professionals working with pupils with learning difficulties in a range of contexts;
- senior managers and those responsible for staff and school development or for developing policy and practice with regard to inclusion;
- students undertaking courses of further professional study in the field of special educational needs.

We hope that it will be read with interest as well as recognition and that it will have the effect of revitalising classroom processes for teachers and learners alike.

How has this book been written?

In this section we wish to give some thought to the ways in which we have approached the issue of exploring teaching and learning for pupils with learning difficulties and to set our work in the context of some of the literature on methods of enquiry. We should first make it clear that this project was initiated and supported by our receipt of the Fulton Fellowship for 1998/99. This provided both the impetus to proceed and the practical possibility of good quality non-contact time for writing, research and reflection. In gathering material for this book, we have worked individually and together in a number of different ways. We have, for example:

- provided an ongoing programme of professional development activities over time in one special school for pupils with severe and profound and multiple learning difficulties, St John's School in Kempston;
- facilitated one-off professional development sessions for colleagues in inclusive and special school contexts;
- contributed to modules within programmes of higher education, working with participants from a range of backgrounds;
- taught, observed practice and acted as mentors to fellow practitioners;
- followed lines of enquiry into the literature;
- talked, debated and consulted with one another and with colleagues about the issues we have raised;

and used all these opportunities as ways of gathering evidence, developing and checking our ideas and furthering our enquiry. This development work, evidence gathering and professional discourse has provided much of the practical material which we have included in this book. In all cases, we have been explicit about our motives; clarified with colleagues our commitment to this project; and sought permission to use anonymised samples of worksheets, planning materials, pupil profiles or direct quotations drawn from informal discussions or the semi-structured interviews (Powney and Watts 1987) which we conducted with the four phase facilitators at St John's School.

We have characterised this work, in our public descriptions of it, as a form of practice-based enquiry focused on fostering improvements in the quality of teaching and learning in particular schools and situations. We present the outcomes of our analysis of practice in these particular situations with the aspiration that they may contribute to a wider debate about the practice of promoting inclusion for pupils with learning difficulties.

The reflective practitioner

This is not a book written by people who are, in any formal sense, professional researchers. Schön (1991) characterises the traditional, hierarchical model of professional knowledge in the following way:

> Researchers are supposed to provide the basic and applied science from which to derive techniques for diagnosing and solving the problems of practice. Practitioners are supposed to furnish researchers with problems for study and with tests of the utility of results. (p. 26)

As the authors of this book, we would certainly see ourselves, in Schön's terms, as practitioners. We have certainly also furnished ourselves with a series of problems which we, along with colleagues at St John's School and in a number of other settings and situations, have been keen to explore. We would therefore see ourselves as practitioner-enquirers grappling with the real problems that emerge from everyday experience in schools. As Schön (1991) says:

> In real-world practice, problems do not present themselves to the practitioner as givens. They must be constructed from the materials of problematic situations which are puzzling, troubling, and uncertain ... Problem-setting is a process in which, interactively, we name the things to which we will attend and frame the context in which we will attend to them. (p. 40)

We endorse many of the interesting words Schön uses here in order to characterise 'real-world practice'. Our work has been 'puzzling, troubling, and uncertain', even when we have been engaged in the naming and framing processes that Schön identifies, much more often than it has been clear and unambiguous. We have learned to embrace and celebrate our uncertainty because we have come to see it as one of the marks of the authenticity of what we are doing. As Robinson (1993) notes, uncertainty and controversy are likely to be among the characteristics of what she calls a 'problem-based methodology'. Robinson argues that the variables which are often 'controlled out' by the scientific researcher may be the very phenomena 'that are most significant to practitioners' decisions about how to act'. To remove these complexities and ambiguities may result in a 'loss of meaning for the practitioner'. This is certainly something we want to avoid. Our work does not therefore provide a neatly packaged relationship between the problem, the experiment and the solution. Indeed, we have learned to become suspicious of any findings that seem to be too tidy and have found ourselves rejecting some of our early models, which offered intellectual and graphical symmetry but failed, in the end, to encompass the untidy complexity of the teaching and learning that we experience in the classroom. As Robinson (1993) notes, a problem-based methodology will be interested in the ongoing process of 'resolving educational problems', rather than simply in finding 'a solution', which can restrict the enquirer to a 'single-loop search for a solution that fits the existing constraint structure of the problem'.

In embracing uncertainty in this way we have failed to generate easy answers, but we are sure that we have moved on. In describing the process of becoming a 'reflective practitioner', Schön (1991) suggests that this entails moving from 'knowing-in-action' (which he characterises as 'the spontaneous behaviour of skilful practice') towards 'reflecting-in-practice'. As one of the phase facilitators at St John's School said, 'sometimes I do things but I don't know what I do and then somebody gives them a name and I realise that's what I'm doing and it confirms my practice . . . I probably do know what I do because I think about it all the time'. Schön states that the reflective practitioner:

> reflects on the phenomena before him, and on the prior understandings which have been implicit in his behaviour. He carries out an experiment which serves to generate both a new understanding of the phenomena and a change in the situation. (p. 68)

In undertaking the work for this book, we have encouraged ourselves, each other and a number of colleagues whom we have persuaded to join us in this endeavour, to behave in precisely the way that Schön describes. As reflective practitioners, we have perceived a problem and set ourselves the task of exploring it. This has entailed a critique of the ways in which such problems are usually framed. Robinson (1993) notes that enquirers using a problem-based methodology will deliberately explore, critique and evaluate 'existing and . . . alternative constraint structures'. There are parallels here with Hart's (1996) approach to practitioner research, which she calls 'innovative thinking'. Hart encourages teachers to 'probe' their 'existing knowledge, understandings and resources' – to challenge and to call into question established ways of conceptualising practice and pupils – in order to 'reach out for new understandings'. In our work we have attempted, along with our co-enquirers, to reframe and restructure the issues as we see them and to undertake exploratory action. In this sense, we have conducted an experiment – or more accurately a number of experiments on a number of different levels. Each of our actions has produced phenomena which Schön (1991) describes as 'unexpected changes which give the situation new meanings'. Schön provides a compelling metaphor for this process when he describes the way in which the 'situation talks back, the practitioner listens, and as he appreciates what he hears, he reframes the situation once again'. This idea of a 'reflective conversation', which 'spirals through stages of appreciation, action, and reappreciation', emerged as another strong theme in our work together. We found ourselves, then, engaged in a form of reflection on, and in, practice which was characterised by uncertainty as a key impetus to enquiry. We came to agree with Schön (1991) that by working in this way 'the unique and uncertain situation comes to be understood through the attempt to change it, and changed through the attempt to understand it.'

Action research and naturalistic enquiry

These notions of change and understanding would seem to mark our work, again in contrast to conventional scientific research, as a form of action research. Fullan

(1991) links the action research model directly to the process of understanding and effecting change in educational settings. According to Robson (1993), action research seeks both to 'understand' a situation and to 'promote change' through the sorts of cycles of planning, action, observation and reflection that we undertook. Robson (1993) also notes that ideas about '*improvement* and *involvement* seem central' to the action research process. Carr and Kemmis (1986) take this insight further. They suggest that action research entails:

> firstly, the improvement of a *practice* of some kind; secondly, the improvement of the *understanding* of a practice by its practitioners; and thirdly, the improvement of a *situation* in which the practice takes place . . . Those involved in the practice being considered are to be involved in the action research process. (p. 165)

All of these were certainly characteristics of our work. As practitioners we were ourselves involved in the enquiry process and, as we shall note below, we also involved numbers of other participants. We set out with the intention of exploring the possibility of enhancing or improving practice and we rapidly found that one of the key elements in this process was the exploration of the understandings and constructs which practitioners bring to their work. We became interested then in the ways in which our enquiry could itself be seen as a means of promoting improvement in three dimensions:

- situational improvement – through changes in classroom practices for teachers and learners;
- contextual improvement – through changes in teachers' understanding, awareness and capacity for reflection;
- institutional improvement – through whole school development.

An awareness of the everyday nature of these contexts or settings prompted us to see our enquiry as 'naturalistic' or, in Robson's (1993) terms, as an example of 'real world' research. Lincoln and Guba (1985) identify a number of other characteristics of natural enquiry which again we would suggest are characteristics of our own work. For example, as enquirers we consistently:

- enlisted the support of other people in gathering data;
- negotiated meanings, understandings and interpretations with those respondents;
- tended to use qualitative methods in preference to quantitative because, as Lincoln and Guba (1985) note, they are more adaptable and sensitive to the complexities of natural settings;
- accepted the intuitive or felt knowledge of participants as making a legitimate contribution to the enquiry alongside other forms of evidence.

As the dialogue developed between us as co-enquirers and between us and other participants in classrooms and during the staff development activities which we undertook as an integral part of our project, we became increasingly focused on the importance of the perceptions and understandings of our co-enquirers. If there is to be change and improvement in an educational institution, then it must begin with the ideas that teachers and learners have about themselves; about one another; and about the processes entailed in teaching and learning.

Robinson (1993) argues that changes in theories of practice are necessary if change is to be non-coercive. She suggests that if practitioners begin to think about their work in different ways then their practice will change, as it were, from the inside. She argues that this kind of change is qualitatively different from the revised practices that are imposed upon practitioners from 'above' or from 'the outside'. According to Robinson (1993), the purpose of a problem-based methodology (PBM) is:

> to contribute to the understanding and improvement of problems of practice. In brief, PBM involves the reconstruction of theories of action which are operative in the problem situation, the evaluation of such theories, including the assessment of their possible causal role in the problem, and, where necessary, the development, implementation and evaluation of an alternative theory of action. Ideally, these stages of inquiry are embedded in a 'critical dialogue' between researcher and practitioner; that is a conversation that is simultaneously critical and collaborative. (p. 15)

We recognise that our work has many of the characteristics of this sort of iterative process, both in the ways in which our enquiry developed in direct response to changes in the practices in which we were interested, and in the sense that our work was shaped by our interactions with one another and with colleagues. Along with uncertainty and the notions of change and improvement, we came to view conversation, or interaction, or critical dialogue between the various participants in the enquiry process and the problem itself as a further key characteristic of our way of working.

Schools as problem-solving organisations

Skrtic (1991) argues that the form of school organisation which he refers to as 'adhocracy' 'is premised on the principle of innovation rather than standardisation'. He also brings together, in his analysis, many of the themes – the value of uncertainty; the driving forces of change and innovation; the power of critical dialogue – which we have identified in our own work. Skrtic states that:

> adhocracies . . . are problem-solving organisations that configure themselves around uncertain work – work that requires the invention of new programs for unfamiliar contingencies through divergent thinking and inductive reasoning on the part of multidisciplinary teams of professionals engaged in a reflective discourse. (p. 35)

Skrtic moves this debate a little further however. He suggests that the creation of adhocracies 'will require an enduring source of instructional uncertainty' and that welcoming pupils with a wide range of needs can provide that uncertainty. As Skrtic says, 'school organisations cannot become and remain adhocratic without the uncertainty of student diversity'.

Ainscow (1991) conceptualises this as the need to 'see pupils experiencing difficulty as indicators of the need for reform'. In thinking about education in this way, schools become 'places where teachers and pupils are engaged in activities that help them to become more successful at understanding and dealing with the problems they meet'. Problems are seen as 'opportunities for learning'. Indeed, Ainscow argues that schools should become 'organisations within which everyone, both pupils and teachers, is engaged cooperatively in the task of learning' and where 'teachers are encouraged to learn from experience and experiment with new ways of working alongside and with their pupils and colleagues'. Within this 'collaborative context for problem-solving', individual teachers should be encouraged to 'take responsibility for the development of their practice'. In order to do this, according to Ainscow 'individual teachers must have sufficient autonomy to make flexible decisions that take account of the individual needs of their pupils and the uniqueness of every encounter that occurs'. In a similar way, our project approaches the issue of school improvement by examining the minutiae of teaching and learning processes.

Ainscow's attitude towards reflective practice has been influenced by the literature on the teacher as researcher; action research; cooperative inquiry; and naturalistic inquiry. Ainscow (1991) provides the following summary of the characteristics of school-based enquiry led by reflective practitioners:

1. Forms of inquiry are used that encourage teachers to examine particular events or processes as a whole and in their natural settings.
2. The design of the inquiry is seen as being emergent; that is to say, the directions and forms of an investigation are decided upon as information is collected.
3. The teacher is seen as the primary 'instrument' for gathering information, using natural methods of information-gathering such as observation and discussion.
4. Wherever possible, inquiry is seen as a collaborative process involving colleagues and pupils.
5. Through processes of data analysis and interpretation, theories emerge from information that is collected. This is usually referred to as 'grounded theory' in that it is seen as being grounded in the data (Glaser and Strauss 1967).
6. Accounts are usually presented as case studies with, where possible, some attempts to suggest tentative applications of the findings to other settings. (p. 13)

The 'grounded theory' to which Ainscow refers emerges from the analysis of individual professional experience. The 'sensitive insights' into practice which Glaser and Strauss (1967) describe may be considered as a form of data and subjected to 'systematic comparative analyses' in order to generate new theory. Stenhouse (1979) also argues that the use of action research should contribute to the development of 'a theory of education and teaching which is accessible to other teachers'. While we would hesitate to claim that this book provides anything as grand as a theory of education, we do hope that it is accessible to teachers and that it will make a contribution to practice.

What is the context for this book?

A central aim of this book is to highlight the unique and critical role played by teachers in the process of teaching and learning within schools. In an attempt to question some of the assumptions surrounding and underpinning the work of teachers, we try to raise awareness of the complexities of the network of conflicting influences which make up daily life in schools. Our approach is to consider different levels of influence, which converge and impinge upon the teaching and learning process. To consider only class-based issues, would, we feel, present a partial view. In an attempt to consider, albeit briefly, influence and expectations at organisation and societal level, we hope to present a balanced perspective of the sources of challenge facing practitioners within the field of education in the current climate of change.

Making sense of life in schools

The way teachers view their work affects not only the quality of their work but also the way they view themselves. Teaching is a stressful occupation. Anxiety is often induced when teachers feel their values and their attempts to serve the interests of their pupils are compromised. Sources of such tension are many but invariably arise when 'teachers are faced with difficult working conditions, a lack of resources, the constant change of rules and the adverse judgements of society' (Tilstone 1991a).

Difficulties at work are often defined by teachers as personal problems. By thinking in this way, staff attribute the cause of these difficulties to themselves. Such difficulties are thus compounded by guilt feelings and consequent lowering of morale. We acknowledge the influence of the sociologist C. Wright Mills in making the distinction and highlighting the causal relationship between 'private problems' and 'public issues'. 'Issues' are beyond the control of individuals and are located within the social world but are frequently defined by participants as private problems, usually with debilitating results. In order to identify the relationship between the public and the private, and by the same token locate the social and political causes of professional dilemmas, practitioners must stand back, reflect and recognise the pervasive processes at play (Wright Mills 1959). We wish, therefore, to reinforce the advice of Garner *et al.* (1995) who state that 'teachers must analyse their personal response to professional situations in order to make sense of what they are participating in.'

This is important for all teachers but particularly so for those who take responsibility for pupils with special educational needs. Teachers within this area of education, despite much good practice, have had to 'contend with the inference that SEN work carries less professional status than, for example, generic subject based work' (Garner *et al.* 1995).

If individuals are able to make sense of the difficulties they face at work they will become better equipped to orient themselves in the teaching and learning process, remain positively focused and ultimately increase their individual and group ability to exert influence and establish control over events. They will thus feel better about their work and consequently feel better about themselves as professionals. Such development and raising of awareness can only enhance conditions conducive to effective change within schools. As Tomlinson (1982) notes:

> If those involved in special education come to think in wider historical, social and political terms about what they are doing, rather than going about their work with a rigid set of procedures loosely labelled 'educational', they will understand more clearly what they are doing, and be able to improve practice. (p. 25)

The political dimension of life in schools

Over the last fifteen years there has been unprecedented pressure from government to instigate radical change throughout the education system. A stream of legislation, discharged at an alarming rate, has affected all aspects of educational provision, procedure and practice. The cumulative effect of such a 'plethora of policies' (Vlachou and Barton 1994) has been to generate acute overload within the teaching profession and cause destabilisation. As Tilstone

(1991a) comments, 'change is necessary, but forced, ill understood attempts to bring about changes are counterproductive and inevitably result in stress at all levels.'

Overload, confusion and instability are not ideal conditions under which to cause meaningful educational change with the aim of improving inclusive practice within schools. Given that effective policies are those that rest upon an articulation of the values and beliefs of the people who must ultimately implement them, we cannot afford to become complacent regarding the challenges presented by inclusion. In relation to the attitudinal effects of the social context of teachers, Vlachou and Barton (1994) caution us that, 'calls for teachers to promote more inclusive educational priorities will be viewed as an additional burden if, for example, they feel insecure, lack encouragement and are provided with little serious, sustained and adequately resourced staff development.'

Not only are mainstream schools expected to cater for increasing numbers of pupils with learning difficulties but schools generally are having to support increasing numbers of teachers with no relevant training in the field. This dilemma is a public issue as would be defined by C. Wright Mills and remains a manifestation of intertwined government policies impacting upon the system over time. The cumulative effects of the demise of initial teacher training in learning difficulties, and the later reduction in in-service training, present a recruitment challenge to schools which are seriously attempting to meet the needs of all pupils. The Teacher Training Agency's competency based framework provides no opportunity for newly qualified teachers to have reflected upon the wider social and political issues inherent within the field of learning difficulties. As Garner *et al.* (1995) note, such a 'lack of understanding or awareness is likely to breed misunderstanding and prejudice.'

The legislative thrust, with its tendency towards centralisation on one hand and increasing delegation to schools on the other, has created a fundamental tension between government prescription and individual teacher autonomy. On the one hand prescription seeks to reduce the teacher to a technician who possesses a specified list of competencies and skills. On the other the reduction of teacher autonomy purports to protect pupils against the 'whims' of teachers who do not know what works. The point to be made here is that no one within the education system knows 'what works'. This point, highlighted by Hargreaves (1999), lies at the centre of our thinking and provides the basic impetus for this book:

> To make teachers more effective at the rate and scale that the government now expects requires practising teachers to be actively involved in the creation of new professional knowledge and in devising new systems for disseminating it to other schools. (p. 17)

Schools must set about making sense of the impending changes proposed by government. Likewise schools must not make unwarranted assumptions concerning the people who are to be involved in the intended changes of ways of working. The new professional knowledge must transcend the transient effects of the package approach to teaching. In order to 'validate' their knowledge, teachers must be innovatory and forward thinking whilst selectively retaining tried and tested professional practice. Above all such practice should be developed and refined through collaboration. As Hargreaves (1999) says,

> Teachers . . . 'tinker' with new ideas, adapting them to make them work or rejecting them when they don't. Teachers become skilled at trialling and improving their professional learning. But they mostly do this on their own; that's the trouble. In schools that are learning organisations teachers tinker together and share ideas and experiences in a constant search for what works better. (p. 17)

A major challenge will be for schools to network and disseminate the resulting professional knowledge in such a way as to ensure change occurs across a diverse range of settings and geographical boundaries. The challenge takes shape when considering that over 30,000 schools are involved which are made up of over half a million teachers. Giving the final word at this point to Hargreaves (1999):

> Raising standards through effective teaching and learning depends on turning schools into knowledge creating organisations that treat teachers as creative but disciplined professionals. Academic research and inspection will always provide part of the evidence base, but there is no substitute for front line practitioners with the commitment and space to undertake the core of research and development on which the improvement of teaching hinges. (p. 17)

The aim of this book is to assist teachers in 'making sense of what they do' and by the same process engage with others in developing and disseminating the professional knowledge of teaching and learning.

How should this book be used?

We hope that this book will provide an impetus for:

- individual reflection, enquiry and development in relation to practice;
- shared debate, shared practices and practice-focused programmes of professional development;
- policy review and policy making.

As we explain below, we regard these dimensions as inextricably linked. We have therefore not divided this text up into a 'practitioner' section, an 'INSET' section and a section for 'managers'. We hope that readers will come to agree with us that the issues we address here are indivisible one from another. We provide a detailed contents page which will help people to find or relocate sections which are of particular interest, but we would encourage all readers to follow all of our debate. We have tried to ensure that the sections of this book offer a balance between theoretically grounded discussion of the issues; descriptions of staff development activities; an analysis of practice linked to the exploration of classroom planning materials; and a review of the implications for policy making and whole school development. We hope that the book will therefore support:

- practitioners in developing a repertoire of effective teaching approaches and in promoting strategies and skills for learning which will benefit pupils with a range of learning difficulties;
- coordinators and managers in promoting a varied and appropriate range of approaches to teaching and learning for pupils with learning difficulties, wherever they are working;
- policy makers in reviewing and developing the relationship between teaching and learning and inclusion.

Our use of terms

In writing this book we have adopted certain conventions in our discussions about the various participants in the teaching and learning process. In talking about colleagues and pupils, we have generally tried to keep to plural forms which are not gender-specific. Where we need to refer to anonymised individuals, we refer to teachers as 'she' and pupils as 'he'.

We intend the term 'teaching' to include the work of all classroom staff who contribute to pupils' learning (for example, teachers, support staff and, in many instances, professionals with a paramedical background). Where relevant, we write about 'staff' and include within that term all such members of the staff team. On occasion we have regarded it as helpful to be more specific about aspects of particular roles and we discuss the work of 'teachers', 'subject coordinators' or 'school managers', for example.

This book is about pupils who are most commonly described in current usage as experiencing learning difficulties. We have used this term because it is convenient and widely understood. We intend our use of this term to include pupils with severe and profound and multiple learning difficulties. Some readers may find that our comments will also have relevance for those learners who are said to experience mild or moderate learning difficulties. Some of the 'pupils with learning difficulties' to whom we refer in this book are, in fact, students who are described as having learning disabilities. We mean our comments to have application across the age range and to include those learners who are still in full-time education beyond the age of sixteen. Where appropriate, we have used terms like 'pupils with special educational needs' (in order to reflect a broader debate) or 'pupils with multi-sensory impairments' (in order to make comments about pupils who have certain specific characteristics as learners). We suggest to readers, on the basis of experience, that all these terms are used to mean different things in different contexts and that they are all problematic as descriptions of real learners.

The following chapter returns to the task of defining terms and explores, in more depth, some of the key issues which we have sought to address in our work for this project.

2 Definitions

In this chapter, we address some of the key ideas with which we will be working in this book including:

- What do we mean by the culture of an institution?
- What do we mean by teaching and learning?
- What do we mean by including pupils with learning difficulties?

In responding to these questions, we focus on the contributions that different members of the school community can make to the creation and maintenance of a 'learning culture'; describe some approaches which we have used in order to support colleagues' discourse about practice; and review the relationship between pupil diversity, inclusion and the process of institutional development.

What do we mean by the culture of an institution?

We might begin by defining the term 'culture' as the shared values, beliefs and understanding inherent within the social relations and working practices of the group. The culture of a school tells us what the school is about, how it functions and the ways in which it treats people. The culture will shape and colour the ethos, and influence the way in which the school sees itself and the way others see it.

Culture is a concept which aids our understanding of human behaviour within organisations and is borrowed from sociology. Schools are organisations and although all schools are different, there are nevertheless features common to all. Likewise, although different from banks and corporate businesses, schools share some significant features or ways of operating that apply to all organisations. Such regularities or ways of working within organisations can help us understand what is going on in our schools and assist us also in promoting positive and effective change. Studying the culture causes us to look at how teachers in a school make sense of life within the workplace. This point is important, as much research concerned with educational change has over-emphasised the 'management of change' whilst understating the 'meaning of change'. This point is succinctly emphasised by Rudduck (1986) who states,

> Radical change in schools and classrooms (i.e. change that profoundly affects the basis of practice) involves change in the culture of the working group. One set of meanings has to be replaced by a new set of meanings, and until the new meanings can be reflected in a set of shared principles that will guide action within the working group, the change in question will be precarious. (p. 107)

The concept of culture can help us identify the necessary and sufficient conditions required to cause effective change in schools resulting in improved teaching and learning in classrooms.

How do 'cultures' vary?

Handy (1985) outlines four cultures which are helpful when looking at schools as organisations. The cultures are 'ideal types' and are not found in pure form, schools being shaped by the differing cultures to varying degrees. The *'club culture'* is present when a strong or charismatic head teacher exerts a pervasive and all-controlling influence over staff. Such a head teacher is reluctant to delegate, shares only selected information and remains very much the visible leader in all areas of activity. The *'role culture'*, in contrast, is where staff discharge clearly delegated and defined duties, and are 'managed' through sets of rules, documented guidelines and detailed procedures. Value is placed upon the role rather than the person. The *'task culture'* promotes collaborative problem solving and functions flexibly in order to face a series of on-coming challenges. Teamwork here is paramount and each member of staff in a given project remains 'first amongst equals'. Finally the *'person culture'* typifies the school in which the individual abilities and skills of staff are valued more than the collaborative or team aspects of the institution.

One can see how the four types resemble broadly differing forms of educational institution. The club culture can be found within the small primary school in which lines of communication are fast and potentially effective. It is an informal and adaptable culture. This culture has flourished within the special school where the head teacher has, until recently, enjoyed more freedom to develop pervasive and personalised managerial styles. The role culture serves very much the needs of the large organisation and is seen operating typically within the secondary school and the exceptional large and complex special school. The role culture is impersonal and bureaucratic in style, responding well to routine tasks but less well to challenges that are new, unpredictable or for which a predetermined answer cannot readily be found within the rulebook.

In identifying the most appropriate culture or blend of cultures, it is first imperative to be clear as to the needs of the school. Given the prevailing educational climate one might reasonably ask which culture will best respond to internal crisis, intense external threat or a series of conflicting messages from authority. While the school needs to have a sound administrative and procedural base (role culture) it may also need to be able to adapt creatively, collaboratively and quickly in response to challenge and change (task culture) in order to develop whilst sustaining a sense of order and indeed sanity.

It would seem that a balanced blend of role and task culture could well serve the development and changing needs of many schools. Role culture ensures that many *maintenance* tasks are undertaken by providing, for example, detailed job descriptions for curriculum coordinators. Such tasks might include:

- production and dissemination of relevant documentation;
- leading in-service training;
- keeping inventories and ordering resources.

The organisational and procedural dimension of the role culture may then be complemented by task oriented project teams. A group of individuals brought together in accordance with their combined knowledge and experience and directed by a clearly defined brief provides a school with a powerful means by which to initiate, monitor or evaluate a particular project. As West (1996) notes, 'this judicious mix of role and task structure has much to commend it and fits well with the responsive, reciprocal features of life in primary schools.'

In order to achieve the aim of generating internal development from external pressure (Fullan 1991) teachers need to understand, as well as simply manage, change. The meaning of change must be translated into the language of the classroom and staffroom if it is to be effective and avoid undue stress and indeed potential disillusionment. This is easy to say but less easy to practise. Schools and classrooms are complex sets of social relations functioning under conflicting pressures. Causing change which entails different ways of thinking and behaving, whilst at the same time 'keeping the show on the road', is a major management challenge for all involved. New ways of working are seldom, if ever, made clear to those in the front line.

What is involved in cultural change?

Moving a school forward will demand internal evaluation of the values and beliefs held by teachers. Two associated and essential elements within this process of school self-evaluation are firstly, *leadership*, and secondly, *staff awareness* at individual and group level. In order to appreciate these two essentials it is useful to consider briefly leadership style and school setting conditions.

Leadership style

Southworth (1998a) notes, 'leadership is concerned with achieving *goals*, working with *people* in a social *organisation*, being *ethical* and exercising *power*.' Within a role culture 'transactional management' prevails. Staff are managed rather than led and procedure predicts practice rather than vision promoting purposeful ways of working. Leadership, within a culture more responsive to challenge, will recognise the individual and organisational needs of staff and seek ways to transform values from within the group. We are describing 'transformational management' as a necessary condition for such cultural change. What does this look like? The head teacher will be an active participant in school-based curriculum development. Further, the head teacher and senior managers are critical players in promoting confidence and self-belief in others. Senior management, through a balance of pressure and support, will encourage and inspire staff to critically question themselves and share ideas about their teaching practice and about pupil learning.

Stoll (1991) outlines how the most effective head teachers adopt a low-profile approach to management, their leadership style being subtle but compelling. In terms of messages, both explicit and implied, the performance of managers must signal to staff a set of practised principles, clear purpose and priority. Decision-making goes with the job and whilst a democratic style actively involves others, the consultative process must not become protracted. An unpopular decision is better than no decision and, if in keeping with practised principles such as equity, will be understood, accepted and respected.

As O'Brien (1998) observes, 'in a management position you cannot be accountable for some aspects of the school and not for others. A collegial and democratic style of management still requires someone to make the decisions.'

The management of information is critical. A conscious, clear and consistent distinction between dissemination and diffusion of information is vital if all are to become involved in the process and genuinely understand what policy and practice means to them as individuals as well as a group (Rudduck 1986). The practical art of conveying or sharing information requires careful consideration in order to avoid 'versions' of policy permeating the organisation with potentially distorting and damaging results. Whilst acknowledging that a management structure is inevitable in any organisation, the head teacher must recognise what particular combination or team of staff best 'fit the job' (Hopkins *et al.* 1996) and are able to facilitate mobilisation and delegation with ease (task culture).

Setting conditions: structure

A balanced blend of structures and processes within a school organisation provides the necessary conditions for effective change in values and beliefs. Most head teachers simply inherit a given management structure with little explanation or understanding as to why it looks the way it does. Many new head teachers, given the opportunity, attempt to change the structure believing it will provide for them a sense of ownership or impose a stamp of originality. But what should the school organisational structure look like? Essentially the form of the structure should be determined by its function. It should reflect three basic overlapping fundamentals. Firstly, the structure should accommodate the diversity of work to be undertaken. This is far from straightforward in a special school and formidable in a large secondary school. The greater the diversity the more complex the organisational structure. Secondly, the structure should provide a firm yet flexible framework for both organisational stability and institutional development. The strength of the structure will determine the school's ability to control change, ensuring it occurs incrementally whilst minimising destabilisation. Thirdly the structure should facilitate the networking of all individuals within all sections of the organisation, from the governors to part-time premises staff. The structure needs to be clear to all in terms of how it practically involves them as individuals in the policy-production and operational life of the school. Only when individuals understand this will they actively contribute towards the overall effectiveness of the organisation. Making structure clear means it must be communicated to all, initially through some form of induction and then through ongoing practical involvement.

With these three fundamentals in place, the structure can work effectively to bring about:

- clarification of roles and responsibilities – reducing potential confusion, conflict and duplication of work;
- clear and effective lines of communication – both top-down and bottom-up;
- meaningful consultation – at every level within the organisation;
- coordination of task allocation, implementation and review – thus providing the operational interface between policy and practice.

The coordinating arm of the structure is vital and must work towards all elements within the organisation operating in a mutually supportive manner thereby reducing sectional or inter-group tension. This can be achieved through scaffolding of coordinating mediums including, for example:

- documented guidelines and procedures – such as the school handbook of information;
- permanent coordinating groups – for example the senior management team or the curriculum committee;
- temporary coordinating groups – like a task-focused working party with an explicit and documented remit or terms of reference;
- department/phase coordinating groups;
- individual coordinators.

Clarity of function is paramount when designing the structure. The aim is to keep the structure as simple as possible whilst accommodating full diversity of work. The temptation will be to 'add on' functions to committees or further extend responsibilities of coordinators in an attempt to make them 'multi-purpose'. This may not be helpful as such add-on may confuse or cause conflict within or between groups or individuals. A clear distinction needs to be made between types of agenda or remit, for example, administration/curriculum, managing/ mentoring and such discrete functions must remain discrete.

It is interesting to note that organisations within the world of business are moving away from hierarchical structures and towards flat structures and networking, essentially in order to sustain responsive and flexible ways of working and to provide individuals with maximum professional autonomy. This points schools in the direction of the task culture if they are to learn from corporate organisational lessons. The management challenge is to generate and channel cultural forces within the school using the relative strengths of each in the right place and at the right time.

Setting conditions: processes

As West and Ainscow (1991) observe,

> we have to be sensitive to the nature of schools as organisations . . . they are about relationships and interactions between people. Consequently a successful school is likely to be one in which relationships and interactions are facilitated and coordinated in order that those involved feel they are engaged in a common mission. (p. 83)

An appropriate organisational structure will allow for planned activities and frequent opportunities for reflection and professional dialogue, which will promote common understanding, change attitudes and improve performance of staff. Such processes, or planned activity, will ensure that staff have regular opportunities to 'clarify concepts, share experience and solve problems together' (Stoll 1991). These planned and incidental activities could be usefully regarded as the school infrastructure and are the means by which the school improves as a direct consequence of teacher development. To aid this necessary process we need to think creatively about staff development and support. It is now well accepted that much 'staff training' in schools has proven largely ineffective in bringing about intended and sustained change (Fullan 1991). Staff development is not and never has been a 'one-stop-shop' providing the 'quick fix'. Schools involved in the 'Investors in People' award scheme will know well that it takes about five years before real change is evident. Change in schools is a slow, incremental and on-going process. Such change is witnessed after prolonged strategic efforts by the organisation towards improving conditions for all in working towards common aims. In order for staff development to function effectively within school, certain conditions are required. As such the staff development process should:

- be clear in its objectives, thus providing a post-training action plan and by the same token specific means of evaluating effectiveness;
- provide effective links between the needs emanating from a teacher's developing role and the priorities within the school development plan;
- be targeted at individuals or a group of individuals identified within the school as change agents, for example a behaviour management support team;
- use external consultants selectively and strategically, for example through cooption to the school's curriculum committee;
- use creatively the school's working environment as a context for development focus, including, for example, regular meeting slots, specific lessons;
- cause teachers to discuss, observe and regard each other's practice as a valuable source of individual and group professional development.

Staff support remains inextricably associated with development but it is useful for planning purposes to regard them as separate strands within the school's policy. Clearly, for new teachers joining the school an induction programme commensurate with role will prove a sound investment. Likewise mentoring and appraisal processes are now commonly regarded as essentials within the educational workplace. Two further staff support systems or processes are less commonplace but no less important. 'Peer coaching' is becoming better understood through its use within organisations operating school-based teacher training programmes. Peer coaching is essentially a teacher possessing particular skills and expertise, assisting and supporting another who is less experienced or skilled. This process of 'teachers teaching teachers' is a powerful and direct means of 'spreading the individual talents of a group of teachers to all so that the team becomes greater than the sum of its parts' (Southworth 1998b).

The second process is that of the 'staff support team.' This is potentially highly effective and has been developed at St John's School in support of staff managing challenging behaviour. Essentially a small group of staff share a combination of skills and knowledge within a particular field. This group receives and cascades targeted training and acts as an advisory or support group to other groups or individual teachers experiencing difficulty. The group possesses a clearly defined remit and is accessed through an agreed referral system. As Creese *et al.* (1998) note, 'American research has indicated that teacher support teams (TSTs) can contribute to a drop in the number of inappropriate referrals to outside services, and other benefits.'

How do we change a culture in order to change a school?

Perceiving organisations as the outward manifestation of cultures allows us to see that there are different ways of arranging things and different ways of doing and reviewing things. If one grows up and develops professionally solely within a single culture it will understandably be difficult to break out of that particular mind-set expressed as those particular ways of thinking and behaving. Knowing there are different ways of working is helpful but not, however, a solution. What do we do to an organisation in order to establish the right conditions required for increasing its potential for improved change?

Figure 2.1 portrays diagrammatically the dynamic interdependence of the different conditions which we have identified as essential for a culture conducive to change. Each corner of the rectangle represents a 'necessary condition'. All four together constitute the 'necessary and sufficient conditions' required for a culture of improvement. As the diagram illustrates, one condition cannot be changed without affecting all the others. One cannot, for example, go about changing staff involvement without considering the processes of staff development and support. The challenge for school management is judging when, how and where to begin. As Handy and Aitken (1986) observe, 'schools probably have more choice than they think they have if they unlock themselves from their conditioned ways of thinking about organisations.'

In summary

This section has made a series of points about the school as an organisation, which are as follows:

• the concept of *culture* assists in understanding change in schools;

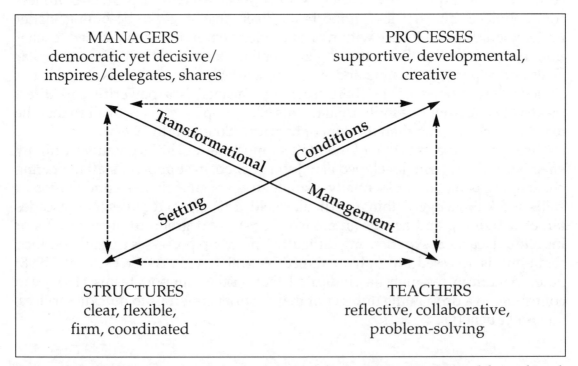

Figure 2.1 The dynamic interdependence of the conditions essential for cultural change

- a balance between *role* and *task* culture may meet the changing needs of many schools;
- *transformational management* is likely to engender real change in schools;
- school organisational structure must be clear to all and accommodate full diversity of work;
- staff development and support systems must recognise and establish links between personal and professional needs of staff and priorities within the school development plan.

What does a 'learning culture' look like?

A willingness on the part of teachers to reflect upon classroom experiences, as well as time for this, are essential for a school to develop and improve its practice. As Southworth (1998b) observes, 'a learning school . . . is not only a place where teachers work but also a place where they learn about their teaching or that of others.' Whereas teachers are confident in talking in meetings about curriculum planning, subject coverage and pupil progress, they are less accustomed or prepared to discuss their own teaching or that of others. Nevertheless, it is becoming clear, as Hopkins *et al.* (1996) note, 'that if the confidence to take a critical and self-critical look at classroom practice can be established, then classroom level enquiry and reflection can do much to increase the quality of learning.'

What then, does a school need to do in order to motivate teachers to develop individually and collaboratively their beliefs, knowledge and skills for teaching? Three school-level strategies can play a significant part in assisting this process.

First, a systematic approach to whole-school development can be adopted in which it is made clear that it is concerned with the development of its staff as well as its pupils. An overall framework, such as that provided by the 'Investors in People' programme, causes all within the organisation to reflect upon whether they are adequately trained and supported to fulfil their particular role and are fully prepared to play their part in meeting school aims. As O'Brien (1998) notes, 'teaching is an intellectually and physically demanding occupation that can be made more effective and efficient when the school accepts the common, distinct and individual needs of staff as well as those of children.'

Secondly, senior management can be seen to be investing in its own professional development as well as valuing and being prepared to invest in the development and learning of all teachers. The idea that 'we are all here to learn' embraces everyone within the school including the head teacher and management team. Managers need to be pursuing recognised training commensurate with their role, for example the National Professional Qualification for Headship or specific skill enhancement related to an area of school priority. Important also are the opportunities which managers create to celebrate their own successes in learning and likewise recognise and share in the celebration of others' learning styles and achievements. As Tilstone (1991a) reminds us, 'senior management, too, will need to be involved in in-service training as teachers and as learners.'

The third strategy is the careful targeting of resources to ensure regular quality meeting time so that teachers can discuss and reflect upon classroom practice and likewise participate in observation and demonstration of teaching. A radical rethink of the school policy on the allocation of 'directed time' may be required, thus redefining the overtly administrative concept of 'teacher planning time'. Such careful channelling of resources could include providing teachers with easy access to various sources of information such as a staff library with Internet facility and regular links with external consultants who are able and 'prepared to support the process of enquiry' (Ainscow and Hart 1992).

Talking about one's own and others' teaching, in any formal way, is clearly not a simple 'taken for granted' activity. Ultimately the structures and processes operating within the school must work at increasing and coordinating the opportunities for teachers to share and work together in small focused groups. Further, the school must set about reducing the level of anxiety which may, for some, be associated with such encounters. As Garner *et al.* (1995) observe:

> it is important to remember that reflection on practice is at its most effective when others are allowed to participate in the process in a supportive way. But, however encouraging colleagues can be, receiving opinions from other teachers about the work we do can be immensely threatening. (p. 12)

For such reasons, management must not only appear to trust and value the developing role played by the 'group' within the organisation but also give serious thought to the size, membership, purpose and systems of its groups in order to coordinate and support structured discussion of teaching. One strategy is to start with the smallest group, the class team, and introduce a supported system of reciprocal observation and feedback activities. A study by Morgan *et al.* (1998) found that a programme aimed at improving the collaborative skills within class teams, emphasising the identification of personal work styles and preferences and self-assessment, proved to be highly effective in achieving its objectives. Central to this programme is reciprocal observation within the classroom. The observer records only factual information set against what has been identified earlier as a 'focus' by the observed. The observer makes no judgements at all, written or verbal. The observation 'report' is then used as an agenda for discussion between the two and to assist the observed to self-assess and set personal targets for development. As Morgan *et al.* state, 'the training programme "Teamwork and Evaluation" put observation and evaluation up front, on the assumption that unless we observe, it is difficult to evaluate, and without evaluation, we can neither improve nor even know what to improve.'

This important point can be taken further by exploring the related problem of accessing knowledge or practices outside one's professional experience. The problem, at its most entrenched, is essentially 'not knowing what you don't know'. Simply reflecting upon one's own current practice will not raise awareness of knowledge outside one's own conceptual framework. As one of the phase facilitators at St John's School said, 'when you have been in any institution for some time you absorb so much you forget what it is you didn't know'. (See Figure 2.2.)

Group processes generating reflective dialogue between practitioners can assist in moving a teacher from position (4) to the preferred position of (2). Likewise the same dialogue will assist a teacher moving from (3) to (1), which is the better position to be in.

Dialogue is essential within schools at all levels. A culture of improvement will generate two recurrent and related questions, which, if managed sensitively, can

(1) Aware of what you know	(2) Aware of what you don't know
(3) Not aware of what you know	(4) Not aware of what you don't know

(adapted from Miller and Watts 1990, p. 45)

Figure 2.2 Positions of awareness

generate coordinated and collaborative activity throughout the school. Such activity will, by its nature, involve all in the learning process.

- Firstly, what do we teachers need to learn?
- Secondly, how do we learn most effectively?

There is direct parallel here between teacher and pupil learning. It is likely that a school at any given time will possess a heterogeneous teaching group. As Garner *et al.* (1995) propose, it may, for example, comprise:

- new teachers requiring induction training;
- experienced teachers requiring extension training;
- teachers returning to the job requiring refresher training;
- teachers changing phase or specialism, for example moving from a mainstream setting to a specialist provision requiring conversion training.

A school which embodies a culture conducive to collaborative improvement will view meeting the staff development needs of this diverse range of teachers as an inspiring challenge. It recognises the differing starting points, backgrounds, and preferred learning styles of its teachers. It seeks to provide opportunities to make effective use of this range and diversity. It openly appreciates that everyone has something to learn and, likewise, that all have something worthwhile to contribute towards the teaching and learning process for both teachers and pupils. Whether expert or novice, all will be valued within this culture.

Given that 'the reality of classroom encounters . . . is created in the minds . . . of people' (Ainscow 1991), it follows that the actual process of 'making sense' of such reality is of central importance. The parallel between teacher and pupil learning highlights further the significance of the structures and processes operating within the school. Such infrastructure remains the essential means by which teachers communicate their subjective views about work. Making objective the reality of the classroom through the process of structured dialogue is a critical aspect of generating a common understanding and formulation of shared values. Clearly, individual mental constructs and personal experiences play an influential part when making sense of novel situations. Apparent inertia or resistance towards accommodating new ways of working may, for example, be a reflection of the different starting position and background of a particular teacher compared to that of others within the group. Such 'apparent' resistance may actually be the outward manifestation of feelings of helplessness and, as such, a rational coping strategy. Raising awareness and sensitivity about this potential 'mismatch' is the first step in the process of recognising a teacher learning need, to be addressed through the supportive network of a collaborative school culture.

A school which embodies a learning culture will build a flexible framework for ongoing focused dialogue. It will provide regular and adequate opportunity for teachers, regardless of professional background, to engage in sharing classroom experiences. Such structured dialogue and group process will facilitate:

- the development of a common language to identify and describe the similarities and differences of a developing repertoire of teaching practices;
- an understanding and acceptance that a consensus of approach emerging from a diversity of views and involved debate is a synergising means of improving practice;
- individual and group ability in perceiving new ways of working as natural and non-threatening consequences of ongoing reflection and dialogue;
- reduction of professional isolation and promotion of personal confidence by way of group problem solving and risk-taking.

O'Brien (1998) summarises the essence of the 'learning culture' when he writes:

> A school should provide systems that are responsive to the needs of individual staff and pupils. This can be done when colleagues meet together regularly to review systems and structures within the school and to reflect upon their practices and responsibilities within them. The process of reflection provides a system of mutual support through the sharing of skills, strategies, feelings and difficulties. An acceptance of a difficulty is a positive step – a teacher should never feel that it is going to be interpreted as the acknowledgement of a failure. When difficulties are identified they should be followed by a collective interest in finding solutions. (p. 111)

In summary

This section has identified the essential processes within a 'learning culture' which may be summarised as:

- staff need to talk to each other about their teaching practice;
- all staff and pupils within a school need to be seen as learners;
- reflective dialogue will emerge within small, coordinated and collaborative groups.

What do we mean by 'teaching'?

One of the tasks required of staff within the 'learning culture' of a school will be to study the concept of 'teaching' and examine the relationship between the teaching and learning processes. In order to put this into a perspective, it would seem appropriate to first address the wider concepts of 'education' and 'curriculum'.

What is 'education'?

The goals of education are many, and the emphasis has changed within special education over the years. Friere (1972) sees learners as being 'critical co-investigators in dialogue with the teacher' which enables them to be more liberated in their learning. This would suggest that the relationship between the teacher/teaching and the learner/learning is a crucial aspect of education for all individuals. Sebba *et al.* (1993) suggest that the concept of 'autonomy' is central to education and that the aim should be the development of 'active, self-determined participation on the part of the individual within her community'. Rogers (1983) talks about giving pupils the 'freedom to learn' which would suggest that the teacher needs to plan activities strategically to maximise possibilities for this and be acutely aware of how to support pupils with thinking and learning in this way. Peter Ustinov is quoted as describing education as the process by which a person begins to learn how to learn. This concept has been recognised since ancient times as is highlighted in the Chinese proverb, 'Give a man a fish and you feed him for a day. Teach a man to fish and you feed him for a lifetime.'

What, though, is actually involved in this? How do we support the pupil in the classroom in achieving these goals and becoming 'co-investigators'? What are the necessary conditions within the classroom for this to take place successfully?

It is the role of the teacher, we suggest, to plan, develop, monitor and evaluate learning situations that will enable pupils to be free, thinking and creative individuals who have a desire to learn. As Robinson (1993) suggests educational practice is 'action informed by beliefs about how to achieve educationally important purposes in particular circumstances'.

Having reviewed the definition of education for the purpose of this book, what is it that makes special education 'special'? Is it so different from mainstream education? Our own view supports that of Tomlinson (1989) who suggests that:

> All education is special education. Every pupil is different from every other in at least some respect, and since this may make a difference to what they get out of any particular teaching approach, the intelligent teacher needs in principle to attend to pupil differences. (p. 31)

What is 'curriculum'?

We suggest that the curriculum includes *all* the learning experience offered by a school. OFSTED (1995) state that the special school curriculum should:

- be balanced and broadly based;
- promote the spiritual, moral, cultural, mental and physical development of the pupils;
- prepare pupils for the opportunities, responsibilities and experiences of adult life;
- include the subjects of the National Curriculum;
- provide for religious education in accordance with an agreed syllabus;
- provide for sex education.

This model of a curriculum is relevant to any school, whether mainstream or special. Historically, the mainstream curriculum, especially that of a secondary school, has been syllabus driven, and the special school curriculum has been needs driven. In order for all pupils' needs to be met within one curriculum, a balance of the two must be developed. The success of this must surely rest on the ability of the school effectively to monitor, evaluate, develop and refine the teaching and learning that is taking place. The curriculum needs to be such that it prepares all pupils for life after school. If the curriculum is to be effective, then the way in which it is taught, and the teacher's ability to meet the individual needs of all pupils, is paramount. The curriculum can be more than a curriculum for life. Through successful teaching and learning it can become a tool for 'living' life, that is, it will provide pupils with the necessary skills, knowledge and attitudes to enable them to make choices and decisions about the ways in which they want to live their lives.

What is 'teaching'?

In Collins English Dictionary teaching is described as:

1. Telling or showing someone how to do something;
2. Giving instructions or lessons in a subject to students;
3. Causing to learn or understand.

This suggests that the teacher is a combination of an imparter of knowledge and a facilitator of learning. It would seem that the concept of education is far greater than the dissemination of the curriculum, but is more to do with the development of independent learners and pupils who are able to think and develop their thinking through a process of self-realisation. Like C.P. Bedford, we suggest that it is the role of the teacher to teach a child to learn by creating curiosity so that he may continue the learning process for as long as he lives. All pupils need to be given the gift of wanting to learn, and in so doing they may grasp every opportunity to enrich their lives.

Hopkins (1997) states that 'powerful learning does not occur by accident but is usually the result of an effective learning situation created by a skilful teacher'. So, what is it that makes a skilful teacher, and how do we ensure that effective learning takes place? It is not simply a question of 'just doing it'; skilful teaching involves a combination of knowledge, skills and attitude that develop over time through training, experience and reflection. It is a practical art that involves the successful integration of teaching and learning. Hopkins (1997) feels that there are three aspects to quality teaching:

- teaching effects, which are described as encompassing sets of teaching behaviours and skills;
- the acquisition of a repertoire of teaching models;
- artistry, which is described as the creative aspect of teaching which involves the ability to respond appropriately and to reflect upon practice.

Harris (1996) suggests that there are then three dimensions of teaching skills that staff should consider:

- knowledge about the subject, curriculum teaching methods, the influence on teaching and learning of other factors and knowledge about one's own teaching;
- the thinking and decision-making which occurs before, during and after a lesson, concerning how best to achieve the educational outcomes intended;
- the action or the overt behaviour by teachers undertaken to foster pupils' learning.

We believe that an effective teacher is a reflective practitioner. Teachers need to reflect upon their teaching in order to refine what they are doing. In relation to this the issue of time needs to be addressed. It is not just a question of what Schön (1991) describes as 'reflection in action'. The school needs to create quality time for teachers to reflect together. This must be planned carefully and staff need to be supported in the development of their team reflection. Tomlinson (1989) suggests that this type of dialogue may be 'threatening' and seem 'irrelevant' to what he describes as a 'closed-minded practitioner', but that a reflective practitioner may find the content of a dialogue 'obvious' once it becomes the highlight of such discussion.

The process of team reflection and effective dialogue enables teachers to develop their expertise and enhances their capacity to meet the individual needs of all pupils whatever their ability. Staff need to be able to create an innate curiosity about learning and about life that will prepare and equip pupils with the knowledge, skills and attitudes to live their lives as they wish within their community. The ability of the teacher in any school setting to recognise and cater for individual differences is crucial. The aims of education are global, not specific to one type of institution alone. This is not an easy process, and there are different pressures and difficulties within educational settings that can inhibit dialogue, for example the numbers of different teachers that one pupil will see over a week in a mainstream secondary school, and the numbers of pupils in a class. We would suggest that each school needs the support and time to engage in dialogue to assist them with this process and move forward according to the needs of their particular establishment.

Exploring the terminology of teaching

When we look at the idea of teaching and the broader concept of education, it becomes very clear that, unlike a natural science, the language of pedagogy is often imprecise. In order for teachers to reflect, share and refine thinking about education in an effective manner, they need to talk the same language. In our experience, this is not currently the case, and in a range of literature different terminology is used freely and with little or no consistency. In some cases the same term is used with different meanings within one piece of literature. Is it any wonder that there is confusion about the concepts of teaching and learning, and staff find it difficult to leave a discussion with the same ideas as their colleagues about what was discussed? Would it not be better for the education of all pupils if staff had a shared understanding of the terminology of teaching? This would enable schools to move forward as a whole rather than as a series of individual parts which may actually be moving in different directions.

Within schools the process of whole staff development should ensure that all staff have a working understanding of the process of education in relation to the aims of the school. Some members of staff will need to be supported in their development of a shared understanding of this process in order that the whole school can move forward together. The new or inexperienced member of staff may help to develop whole team thinking and evaluation through the need to clarify for them the thoughts of more experienced staff. We suggest that having staff who are at different stages of their own learning development actually enhances the monitoring, evaluation and development processes of the whole team and enables a school to become stronger than the sum of its parts.

In the discussion that follows we do not claim that we have a definitive description of what the terminology of teaching should be. However, we do believe that the process of discussing educational terminology as a staff within a school or college will help those involved to develop and move forward together.

The activity we used to develop our understanding of the language of teaching involved analysing the terminology that appeared most frequently in recent educational texts. This terminology included:

- teaching model;
- teaching approach;
- teaching methods;
- teaching strategies;
- teaching skill;
- teaching style.

These terms are not hierarchical in any way, but rather have an integral relationship with each other as part of the whole concept of 'teaching and learning'. It is not possible to look at teaching in isolation without considering the impact of teaching on learning and vice versa.

We asked staff to define these terms individually, and then to discuss them either in pairs or in small groups. Staff then reported back to the whole group, and extensive discussion took place. Colleagues' views and individual interpretations of the terminology shaped people's ideas and conclusions. The activity caused much discussion and deliberation, provoking reflection, both at the time and afterwards. It was only through having these discussions that staff began to use the language more naturally in following discussions related to teaching and learning. It caused people to analyse what they were doing, and to share this through the use of a common language and a common understanding of that language. We would say that this has enabled us to move forward in a more effective manner with the development of teaching and learning in individual establishments and in the work described in the rest of this book.

Having used this activity with a variety of groups of staff, we explore below the common ideas that were discussed in response to each term.

Teaching model

In response to the idea of 'teaching model', staff in a range of institutions generated ideas which included the following:

- a broad based philosophy with a theoretical underpinning and a prescribed range of techniques, for example, Conductive Education, Intensive Interaction;
- a philosophy which dictates approaches and methods and is usually presented as a whole package, for example, Montessori, Froebel, Steiner;
- a description of a set of styles and suggested teaching practices which prescribe how pupils are taught, for example, TEACCH.

As a result of this activity there seemed to be a consensus, both within a single establishment and between establishments, as to what could be meant by this term. It was felt that a model had a broad theoretical base and was aimed at a particular group of pupils, for example TEACCH as a model for pupils with autism, and Conductive Education as a model for pupils with cerebral palsy. These particular models were described as being very prescriptive and designed to be specifically pertinent for a particular group of pupils. Although each model is based on varying educational principles and philosophy, contributors to this activity suggested that aspects of each model could be used in relevant ways in order to meet the specific learning needs of a range of individual pupils.

Teaching approach

In response to the idea of 'teaching approach' participants in our professional development sessions recorded ideas which included the following:

- a broad philosophical idea or standpoint through which teachers individually or collectively arrive at agreed 'tactics' for the education of their pupils;
- a personal philosophy and way of working that underpins teaching and may be dictated or influenced by subject content, age and ability of pupils, individual style, values and beliefs;
- different ways of approaching subjects and delivering the curriculum, for example geography can be formal and art can be more experimental;
- the structure, organisation and content of lessons derived from schemes of work;
- providing the right climate for learning;
- a way to begin and introduce ideas.

This term provoked the most discussion and confusion amongst staff. It meant very different things to different people, and there was not really any consensus reached, although some very similar ideas were explored. It was generally agreed that an approach, like a model, was broad, and that it came from an overriding philosophy. The idea of a sliding scale of approaches was suggested, with extreme behaviourism at one end of the scale, and extreme interactionalism at the other. All 'approaches' that teachers selected would then fall somewhere between the two extremes on this scale.

Owing to the ambiguity of the term 'approach', and the frequency of its use within the English language, we felt that for the sake of clarity of discussion and shared understanding within an educational establishment, we should think very carefully about how we used it. Our agreed definition of 'teaching approach' in terms of how we shall use it for the purpose of this book and how we currently use it within our own work is 'a generic term embracing a variety of related concepts'.

Teaching methods

Respondents raised a number of issues in relation to the idea of 'teaching methods', including the following:

- a way of doing something, which could be followed stage by stage and used by any teacher – for example the short term plan;
- the organisation and implementation of a particular lesson incorporating defined models, approaches and strategies and influenced by subject content;
- a range of possibilities from which staff make decisions about ways of working: for groups and classes; and based on programmes of study and schemes of work.

Discussion around this term involved comparison with a recipe, the method being the way you carried out the lesson following a detailed plan, but affected to some degree by the personal style of the teacher. Staff generally felt that it was related to short term lesson plans, and that it described the transference from medium term plans or schemes of work to a plan that differentiated the curriculum for individual pupils, incorporating individual education plans (IEPs).

Teaching strategies

Participants in our professional development sessions responded to the idea of 'teaching strategies' in a range of ways which included the following:

- consciously structuring and applying the method through your teaching to create learning opportunities for all pupils;
- thinking about and applying knowledge of individual pupil learning processes to your teaching;
- planning prior to the lesson, or undertaken spontaneously within a lesson, in response to pupil reaction and feedback;
- methods specifically employed in organising and working with groups, including presentation of resources, demonstration and discussion;
- altering or adapting the teaching methods and styles already in use, a range of organisational techniques which ensure pupils' access to the curriculum.

Strategies were seen to be the techniques that were used within a lesson in order to meet the individual needs of the pupils. They could be planned prior to a lesson, and may be incorporated into a lesson plan, or could be used within a lesson in response to pupils' reactions to the activity to ensure the involvement and participation of all pupils. It was felt that the uses of these unplanned strategies were decided upon by the teacher based on prior experience, and knowledge of the pupils and subject material.

Teaching skills

Staff involved in this discussion listed what they believed to be skills that were needed for teaching. These included:

- classroom management;
- forming and maintaining relationships with staff and pupils;
- personal and team skills;
- professional skills, such as signing, use of augmentative communication systems, knowledge of subject, observation, assessment, recording.

These were seen as a vital part of the successful implementation of all lessons. Teaching skills were seen as being learned through training and experience, and utilised in order to maximise the learning potential of the lesson.

Hopkins *et al.* (1997) list a range of conditions that are necessary for learning to take place, the skill of the teacher being in implementing them. These are: authentic relationships; boundaries and expectation; planning for teaching; teaching repertoire; pedagogic partnerships and reflection on teaching.

Teaching style

Discussion in professional development sessions with a number of staff developed these notions of what is meant by 'style':

- a way of delivering the curriculum which can be employed to teach a part of the curriculum or a lesson;
- individual ways of adapting teaching methods, approaches or strategies that are affected by the teacher's personality;
- those characteristics or personality traits of the teacher that impact on the way in which something is taught.

These were seen as being an integral part of the implementation of all teaching models, approaches, strategies and methods. Style was seen as being the personalisation of the lesson by an individual teacher, and it was felt that two teachers could follow the same lesson plan, but deliver it in different ways depending on their own particular style.

In summary

In this section we have used examples from professional development activities in order to consolidate a number of ideas about the language of teaching including the following:

- crystallising thinking as a team supports whole-school development;
- developing a common understanding of the concept of teaching and its impact upon the classroom and therefore the pupils is vital;
- reflection, sharing and refining thinking as a team, using a language that is understood and shared by all, develops a common understanding, affects our practice in the classroom and creates new learning opportunities for pupils.

If this way of thinking and working can become part of the culture of the institution, we suggest that it can help to promote an exciting and meaningful education for all pupils and the accelerated development of the school.

What do we mean by 'learning'?

Learning is defined in the Oxford English Dictionary as being the acquisition of knowledge through study, experience or being taught. Sugden (1989) elaborates on this, saying 'learning is seen as an active process with the successful learner being able to retain a skill over a period of time and use it flexibly in a variety of situations.' This reflects our own concept of the curriculum as being a curriculum for life and living, rather than one that has little function beyond the here and now. But what is 'learning acquisition' or the 'learning process' and how do we facilitate it?

An understanding of learning theory would seem to be important to support a deeper understanding of pedagogy. Views on learning theory have evolved over the years. There is now a more eclectic view of how we learn and we have moved beyond seeing learning theory in terms of rats, dogs and pigeons. The words that repeatedly appear within recent educational texts related to learning are 'style', 'strategies', 'skills' and 'processes'. These are therefore the terms that we will concentrate on, and in doing so attempt to reach a joint understanding of what is meant by those terms.

What is 'learning style'?

Learning style is generally defined as the way in which individuals prefer to learn. Riding and Rayner (1998) suggest that there is confusion within the field of education over what is meant by learning style and its crucial role in pedagogical practice. This terminology too needs to be clarified. The clarification process may then assist in teaching a class of pupils with a range of learning styles, knowledge and skills in such a way that learning opportunities are maximised for every pupil in the class.

The whole concept of learning style and its impact on actual learning is huge. Different authors propose varying numbers and kinds of learning style, suggesting that people fall into different categories of 'learner'. Butler (1995, 1997) for example, argues that learners may be 'realistic', 'analytical', 'pragmatic', 'personal' or 'divergent' in style and suggests that individuals may fall into one of these categories or may combine two or more of them. Griggs (1991) defines learning style as the 'composite characteristic cognitive, affective and physio-logical factors that serve as relatively stable indicators of how a learner perceives, interacts with, and responds to the learning environment.'

This would suggest that learning style is at least partly inherent. It cannot be denied that people do learn in different ways, and that individuals have learning preferences. We recognise the reality that some learners like to become quickly engaged in practical activity. Others prefer to consider their options before getting involved. Some pupils demand plenty of adult support and guidance. Others are most at ease when working alone. We return to these ideas and discuss ways in which pupils may be helped to recognise their own learning styles in Chapter 4.

The cognitive centred approach described by Riding and Rayner (1998) outlines the way learning style affects the organisation, processing and repre-sentation of information that take place during learning and thinking. Their work suggests that style may be developed, or that individuals have at their disposal a combination of styles rather than purely one style of learning. This concept would certainly make the whole idea of what learning is about more digestible and easy to understand. Despite its complexity it seems clear that learning style affects our way of being within a learning situation and what we take to and from a learning situation.

The concept of style suggests individual differences as well as similarities in learning preferences. Whether learning style is partly inherent or can be learned, it would seem paramount that the range and variety of learning styles present within our classrooms be recognised and nurtured. By examining style in more detail we may be able to improve the quality of teaching and learning within the classroom.

Learning style: instructional preferences

It would be logical to assume that if people have a particular style or way of learning, then they will have particular instructional preferences that suit this style. Hamblin (1981) highlights what can be considered as the danger of attempting to teach or impose learning style, saying: 'to try to impose a learning style is the pedagogic equivalent of imposing a false self upon someone – an act which is inevitably as destructive in the long run.' Butler (1995, 1996, 1998) highlights the importance of matching the planning of teaching to knowledge of learning style, stating that 'if the learning process engages your style, you are more easily successful as a learner.' Realistically, the pupils will not always be in situations where the experience and the lesson content match their individual learning style. Teachers must look at the development of style that may enable a pupil to learn despite the mismatch. The challenge of being in that situation, if handled sensitively and appropriately by the teacher, may also be a very valuable learning experience for the pupil, encouraging him to learn despite a challenge to his style.

How easy is it, however, to engage the styles of all pupils in the real context of the classroom? How can a varying range of pupils be taught strategies that will enable them to continue to learn even when there is mismatch between the teaching environment and personal learning style? The more strategies that a pupil can learn to use, the more able he will be to make valuable use of every learning opportunity. It would seem then, that we are not trying to 'teach' style, rather to support the development of hybrid strategies that will help the learner be more adaptable and flexible in his learning.

It would seem obvious that if individual pupils' learning styles can be recognised then teaching can be planned to make the most effective use of materials and presentation. Teaching cannot purely happen according a teacher's own learning or teaching style; opportunities need to be provided for all pupils within the class to learn meaningfully from the curriculum. The teacher needs to look at her own teaching strategies and the acquisition and development of learning strategies for her pupils that will enable all to access the curriculum. There may be limited accessibility for pupils with learning difficulties who can have problems with adaptability. The teacher may then need to look more closely at the processes involved in the learning situation, and concentrate on supporting the pupil with the development and refinement of a broader selection of learning processes. Schön (1991) describes this process saying teachers need to acquire 'suitable combinations that will *match* requirements: different types of learning/teaching processes may be needed for different types of competence outcome, for learners with differing characteristics by way of ability, specific experience, cognitive style, motivation.'

Learning strategies

Strategies are the means adopted to enable a person to cope when learning situations do not directly complement personal style. Riding and Rayner (1998) define strategies as 'ways which can be learned and developed to cope with situations and tasks, and particularly methods of utilising styles to make the best of situations for which the styles are not ideally suited.'

They also state that strategies involve a conscious decision to implement a skill. The strategies a person chooses to adopt will be predetermined by previous knowledge, level of understanding and ability. New strategies can be taught that will support the pupil in his learning development and provide the ability to learn successfully in a class of people with differing learning styles.

Baron (1978) offers a learning strategy hierarchy which describes the different types of strategies that may be used:

- *Relatedness search strategies* – actions aimed at defining a new problem in reference to previous knowledge.
- *Stimulus analysis strategies* – actions aimed at analysing a task and breaking it down into its constituent parts.
- *Checking strategies* – actions aimed at controlling and evaluating responses to the learning task in order to arrive at an appropriate response.

Kirby (1984) and Nisbet and Shucksmith (1986) explore this concept and suggest that strategies may operate at different levels:

- micro-strategies, like asking questions and planning, are task specific; relate to previous knowledge and current abilities; and are teachable;
- macro-strategies, such as monitoring, checking, revising and self-testing, are generalisable and subject to development but are more difficult to teach directly;
- central strategies are concerned with broad approaches, attitudes to learning, personal motivation and 'planfulness'.

In order for all pupils within a classroom to learn the most from every activity the teacher needs to consider all levels of strategies. Referring to White and Haring's hierarchy of skills (1980), the teacher needs to consider:

- teaching the actual strategy through demonstration;
- providing the pupil with the skills to practise and refine taught strategies and therefore maintain his skill in using that particular strategy;
- supporting the pupil in using that strategy in other situations;
- providing him with opportunities to adapt them to other situations.

As we have seen, 'micro-strategies' like these can be taught. The teaching of 'macro-strategies' is more complicated as it needs to be geared towards the individual's learning style. In order to teach these strategies, it is therefore paramount that the teacher has a detailed knowledge of the individual's learning style profile (see Chapter 4). With this knowledge she can set up situations that enable the pupil to develop and refine strategies for himself. This may take a certain amount of self-reflection in the form of looking at what has and has not worked in the past, and analysing and utilising the pupil's strengths as outlined in their learning profile. This process can be supported and strengthened with dialogue between professionals working with a particular pupil.

Weber (1978 and 1982) developed a pedagogy and curriculum model which was constructed around the idea of teaching 'efficient learning' strategies, including the following:

- attending to detail;
- identifying starting points;

- establishing and testing hypotheses;
- forward planning;
- systematic exploratory behaviour;
- reasoning and deducing;
- divergent thinking.

Some of these strategies are easier to teach, and some are reliant on a certain level of cognitive ability and on personal learning style. The role of the teacher is to present activities that teach the prerequisite skills for these strategies at the right level for the individual pupils. She needs to be clear as to the pupil's level of understanding and ability, and not present tasks that are outside of the pupil's capabilities. In doing this it is important that she remembers to challenge the pupil without having expectations that are set too high. As Hopkins *et al.* (1997) state, 'There is a central dilemma that faces any teacher faced with a class. Put simply it is this: *how do I work with the whole group and, at the same time, reach out to each member of the class as an individual?'*

Learning skills

Skills are things that we are able to do and are a practical demonstration of knowledge. Skills are usually measurable and can be assessed and reviewed within an individual education plan (IEP). Many published assessments schedules provide a developmental analysis of skill based learning, but the drawback of such schedules is that they do not address the other aspects of learning that are not so easy to measure. White and Haring (1980) describe a hierarchy of levels of development of skills:

- acquisition – in which pupils learn correct new responses through methods such as demonstration, modelling and physical prompting with an emphasis on developing accuracy;
- fluency – in which pupils, through repeated 'doing', reach a level of 'mastery' combining speed and accuracy;
- maintenance – in which pupils consolidate and maintain a high level of competency and fluency over time by 'overlearning' through repetition and familiarity;
- generalisation – in which pupils develop and achieve 'mastery' in different settings or contexts and with different stimuli or materials;
- application or adaptation – in which pupils discriminate key elements of new situations and select appropriate responses, adapting their established skills and understandings to new problem solving opportunities.

Some skills are dependent on prior learning, in other words, the learner needs to have mastered one skill in order to learn another. It can be argued that the practice and maintenance of skills could support the development of those aspects of learning that are more difficult to measure, such as attention, motivation or memory. The application of these new skills in different situations, or in White and Haring's terms, the 'adaptation' of skills, can support problem solving, self directed learning and self motivation. Brake *et al.* (1986) describe a framework of skills that they see as effective tools for learning:

- thinking forward;
- thinking about finding information;
- thinking about using resources;
- thinking about recording information;
- thinking about using information;
- thinking about communication;
- thinking back.

Under each of these headings they look at what decisions need to be made and what skills are required in order to learn successfully in these areas.

As Feiler and Thomas (1988) suggest, skill-based learning only works with frequent practice, and it does not necessarily improve what they describe as 'academic skills'.

The term 'study skills' is used differently in educational discussion and refers to a person's ability and willingness to learn. A selection of study skills needs to be acquired or taught to support learning in a range of situations. Individuals may have a different set of learning strengths and weaknesses, and therefore will require an individualised package of study skills to suit a particular way of learning. Orientation to study may also be affected by particular abilities, disabilities and personality traits. Some examples are as follows.

Capability for using long and short-term memory

Opportunities need to be provided for practising and developing use of long and short term memory. As discussed earlier, practising skills will enable better use of them, and develop the ability to adapt those skills for other circumstances. Memory training activities can be provided either in a purist form, such as games like Kim's Game, or within planned activities where work is reviewed and pupils are encouraged to remember what they have done either within a particular lesson, a space of time, or during the day.

Ability to learn through communication modes such as writing, pictures, the spoken word

Pupils' preferences need to be assessed in learning through particular communicative mediums. Do they work best with writing or pictures to support their learning, and how much or how little, and in what ways should oral language or signed language be used to meet the particular learning needs of the pupils?

Ability to retain attention to task

Attentions span varies from pupil to pupil and from task to task but what can be done to insure that every pupil has work presented in such a way that it holds his attention, and that the classroom environment is conducive to maintaining attention?

Fine and gross motor coordination skills and visual and auditory skills

Every activity that is planned, and the classroom environment, must take into consideration the gross and fine motor needs, and the visual and auditory needs of the pupils. It must also be structured in such a way that it encourages and supports the development of skills in these areas when and where necessary.

Level of understanding of language/communication skills

Staff should have detailed knowledge of each pupil's receptive and expressive language and communication skills. Then the language that is used within a lesson can be understood at every level of ability, and new language can be introduced into an environment that is receptive to building on current knowledge and understanding. Each pupil should have language/communication objectives that clearly set out what he is working on and how to develop these skills. Systems and resources need to be in place that exactly match and support the requirements of those objectives, alongside prescriptive guidelines as to how they should be used by both the pupil and staff. Language/communication profiles can support such programmes and can clearly describe present and potential skills, as well as the resources required to implement these programmes.

Motivation

Different things motivate different people, but if a teacher can discover what motivates the pupils in her class, she will be able to plan tasks that meet the motivational needs of those pupils. If a pupil is motivated by a lesson then he is likely to learn more from that lesson. A teacher needs to inspire in pupils a desire to learn, and that can only happen when motivation is there. As one of our phase facilitators said, 'you can stand and teach until you drop dead, but you can't make somebody learn if they are not willing to learn or you are not sufficiently sensitive'.

Organisational skills

The teacher needs to first look at her own organisational skills: the practical organisation of the classroom and learning resources, and also the organisation of teaching and learning in the planning and implementation of the curriculum. Organisation is paramount in effective classroom practice. An organised teacher can then support the pupils in the organisation of their own learning and thinking, and can teach them how to develop their own organisational skills.

Self-assessment skills

It has been said that the object of teaching is to enable the pupil to get along without the teacher, and in order to do that pupils need to develop self-assessment skills. If education is about learning to live life, then self-directed learning is essential. In order to measure success of learning and evaluate that learning in context, one needs to be able to look critically at what has happened. This is not easy for anyone to do, but if teachers can enable a pupil to self-assess, then they are one step further towards helping him to live his life.

Planning for teaching and learning therefore needs to incorporate emphasis on training and teaching pupils to maximise their abilities in all of these areas.

Learning processes

Sugden (1989) describes the cognitive processing skills that he considers to be involved in the 'learning process' as:

- the selection of detail to attend to;
- the holding of information in some working memory;
- the comparing of incoming information with that held in a permanent store;
- the generating of a plan of action;
- the implementation of this plan;
- the use of feedback.

This analysis might cause us to ask further questions. How does the learner know which aspects of a task to attend to, and what if he selects the wrong detail and therefore 'learns' something different from the task than the intended outcome, which might distort his understanding of a particular concept? How does the learner hold information in his memory, and is it the same for everyone? How does the learner know what information to compare with the current piece of learning? What if he compares it to something else, and again arrives at a different learning outcome that skews his understanding of that concept? What skills does he need to possess in order to generate a plan of action and develop strategies for its implementation? When discussing these questions with a range of staff in a number of different settings, they were simplified to incorporate:

- communicative processes;
- analytical processes;
- sensory processes;
- spatial processes;
- interpersonal processes;
- intrapersonal processes;
- practical processes;
- musical processes.

These ideas, drawing on work by Gardner (1993a) and Mulligan (1992), are described and discussed further in Chapter 4.

Assessment of skills, style and strategies

Assessment of a pupil's skills enables a teacher to see where he is functioning within different areas of development and understanding. There are many published assessments that can support the measurement of these skills, although these are dependent on pupils following 'normal' patterns of development. An individual education plan (IEP) should outline in specific terms the next stage for a pupil and how that will be taught. The IEP should reflect the actual learning needs of the pupil in terms of objectives that have relevance to the statement, when a pupil has one, and incorporate lifelong learning skills that support the cultural and individual needs of the pupil. The subject curriculum objectives should be supported by the IEP objectives, but should be identified and reported on separately.

As has already been discussed, skills are easier to measure, assess and plan objectives around, but assessment of style is not as clear-cut as this. The published learning style profiles demand a certain level of understanding and skills from the person being assessed. How then do we recognise and assess the learning style of a pupil for whom these types of tests are difficult to use and therefore not relevant? We have found that the pupil profile sheets that are described in Chapter 4 assist us in recognising pupils' learning styles. It is through the process of dialogue with such activities that staff can define precisely and develop their understanding of how particular pupils learn. This can then support the decision as to which particular ways of teaching would best suit a pupil, and which processes would need to be highlighted to plan teaching and learning objectives that will give the pupils more developed skills in those areas.

In summary

In this section, we have explored the concept of learning in relation to teaching and established the following ideas:

- learning is complex and the role of the teacher is to facilitate development of all areas of learning that will enable pupils to make sense of and have an impact on their world for their lifetime;
- staff need to encourage independent learning and develop in pupils a hunger for learning that will enable them to see all experiences as learning experiences;
- staff need to heighten their awareness and understanding of themselves and their pupils as learners in order to promote successful inclusion for pupils with learning difficulties;
- teaching is a practical art that demands of the teacher the ability to make every learning experience valuable and worthwhile for each pupil;
- in order to support the development of individual skills, strategies and processes the teacher needs to know each pupil as an individual learner;
- the teacher needs to enable the pupil to see himself as a learner and must equip him with the necessary skills, knowledge and attitude to be a lifelong learner.

Within the context of a special school or a primary school where teaching tends to be class based, the teacher has more opportunity to have an in-depth knowledge of each pupil within her class. This will be affected by class size, mix of year groups and pupil diversity. Individual institutions need to devise ways of working which meet the demands and needs of their own establishment. Within the mainstream secondary school, where some teachers may only meet particular pupils once a week, this process is far more difficult. Schools need to reflect upon their culture and develop the processes required to gain knowledge of each pupil's learning profile. This would support the planning of differentiated lessons that meet the learning needs of all pupils.

What do we mean by 'including pupils with learning difficulties'?

It is salutary to remember that many of the learners with whom we are concerned in this book would not have received a formal education at all prior to 1971. During the third quarter of this century, the distinction between 'two sorts of children, those who are handicapped and those who are not' (Tilstone 1991b) was based upon intelligence quotient (IQ). Pupils with an IQ of less than 50 were considered to be 'severely subnormal' (SSN) and therefore unable to benefit from school. The merely 'subnormal', with measured IQs of between 50 and 75, did go to school, although they were likely to receive their 'special' education separately from the majority of 'normal' learners.

By the time of the Warnock Report (DES 1978), all pupils had been officially considered to be educable for some seven years. Many authors had argued on behalf of the educational needs of pupils with learning difficulties (Stevens 1971) and some commentators had begun to challenge the supremacy of the IQ test as a reliable predictor of educational aptitude (Segal 1967). Debate began to turn upon the question of where pupils with learning difficulties should best be taught.

Integration and inclusion

Starting in the 1970s, and lasting on through the 1980s, there was an impetus towards equity and equality of opportunity, building upon the recognition of the right of all children to receive some kind of education. The Warnock Report and the ensuing Education Act (DES 1981) rejected the notion of hard and fast categories of types of learning difficulty or disability in favour of a concept of a continuum of special educational need. It was acknowledged that pupils within this continuum might have their needs met in a range of possible settings. In addition to the provision established in special schools, various types of integrated provision were discussed and advocated, including:

- locational integration, where children with special educational needs were physically placed in mainstream schools for all or part of the teaching week, although they may have been receiving a separate education;
- social integration, where interactions between pupils with special educational needs and their mainstream peers were facilitated, for example, during play time, meal breaks or during lessons like art, music or physical education;
- functional integration, which encompassed full participation for pupils with special educational needs in shared learning activities and experiences.

As this values-driven movement gathered pace and special schools sought to create closer links with their mainstream counterparts during the 1980s, a variety of integration projects sprang up, often relying on tenuous links between individual members of staff or upon unstable measures of goodwill. In practice, integration at this time tended not to be seen as a radical alternative to special provision. It was viewed rather as a means of reducing the segregation of pupils with special educational needs if a number of practical criteria were met – for example, will the educational progress of the majority of learners in the mainstream classroom be compromised? are there resources available to support this proposed practice? Many integration initiatives therefore entailed the partial relocation of some pupils with special educational needs into 'host' schools under certain carefully controlled conditions – a change of context which entailed little challenge to prevailing concepts or constructs. As Sebba and Ainscow (1996) point out, such integration projects tended to be about 'how to assimilate individual pupils with special educational needs into existing forms of schooling' by: adapting the curriculum to meet the needs of individual or small groups of pupils with special educational needs; devising different work for these pupils within a mainstream setting; or providing support.

The 1990s began to see a change in the language used to describe the processes of desegregation and the introduction of a new set of concepts. The Salamanca Statement (UNESCO 1994) promoted the idea of mainstream schools contributing to the development of an inclusive society by catering for all pupils as a right. In 1996, the Tomlinson Report (FEFC 1996) recommended that colleges of further education should move towards inclusion by 'embracing students with learning difficulties and/or disabilities fully and unequivocally within the general approach to learning appropriate for all students'. Tomlinson argued that the 'concept of inclusion is not synonymous with integration. It is a larger and prior concept.' Inclusion, according to Tomlinson, involves 'redesigning the very processes of learning, assessment and organisation so as to fit the objectives and learning styles of the students' (FEFC 1996).

Other commentators agree with Tomlinson's assertion that inclusion is more radical, as an idea and as a practical process, than integration. Sebba and Sachdev (1997), in their review of international research into inclusion, state that:

> inclusive education describes the process by which a school attempts to respond to all pupils as individuals by reconsidering and restructuring its curricular organisation and provision and allocating resources to enhance equality of opportunity. Through this process, the school builds its capacity to accept all pupils from the local community who wish to attend and, in so doing, reduces the need to exclude pupils. (p. 9)

New meanings

Building upon this notion that schools will be willing to reinvent themselves in order to become more inclusive and less exclusive, Clark *et al.* (1997) define inclusion as 'a new and radical reconceptualisation of the relationship between the education of children "with special educational needs" and the nature of mainstream schools'. It is interesting to note here that not only are schools urged to reconsider their roles, their images of themselves and their practices, but readers are urged, by Clark *et al.*'s use of inverted commas, to reconsider the meaning and value of terms like 'special educational needs'. We are now at some distance from the confident use of terms like 'subnormality' and the consequent prescription of educational opportunities on the basis of an IQ test. There has been a significant move away from deficit-orientated models based on one-dimensional analysis. These can lead to simplistic thinking, whether of the 'within child' or 'social construct' persuasion. Practitioners are no longer certain that pupils' needs can be ascertained solely from a medical description.

We are acutely aware of the negative effects of the medical model. At the risk of political incorrectness we are, however, concerned that an absolute social construction model denies ontological status to any learning difficulty and by so doing denies the existence of very real pupils with real learning difficulties. Some commentators (Cooper 1999) would argue that learning difficulties entail complex interactions between biological, social and psychological influences. Others suggest that in the process of moving towards inclusion, nothing can be taken for granted, neither the nature of mainstream schooling nor, as Hart (1996) and Clark *et al.* (1997) demonstrate, the notion of pupils having 'special educational needs'. We contend that there are objectively verifiable physical factors that impinge upon pupils' learning. We acknowledge the value of the insights which understandings about these factors can bring to classroom practice. A developed body of knowledge exists in relation to, for example, Down's Syndrome or pupils who are deafblind, which if used sensitively and with understanding, can serve to liberate pupils with learning difficulties. We aim to move beyond simplistic rhetoric into the realm of informed practice.

In this book, however, we welcome and celebrate a measure of conscious uncertainty about the descriptions which are applied to pupils and used in order to define and determine practice. We contend, with Skrtic (1991), that schools and classrooms should be 'problem-solving organisations that configure themselves around uncertain work'. We would argue that the labels which professionals, and often parents, attach to pupils should be regarded as unreliable and subjected to constant re-evaluation and challenge. We would suggest that fixed notions about the nature of schooling are equally unhelpful and undesirable.

It is instructive, perhaps, to recall the introduction of the National Curriculum into schools and the impact that this had upon established notions of curriculum, schooling and learners. Despite the rhetoric proclaiming *A Curriculum for All* (NCC 1989), many schools used the new curriculum framework as a gatekeeping strategy, or even as a spur for exclusion. Some mainstream schools began to argue that certain pupils were unable to engage with the new curriculum on offer, and therefore began to reject those pupils on the basis that, as learners, they failed to conform to the established school model. Many special schools developed similar arguments about the inaccessibility of the National Curriculum for pupils described as experiencing learning difficulties, and rejected the curriculum model. It took many years, much debate and some modifications to statute and guidance to establish the principle that a curriculum framework within which all pupils can flourish as learners has to be flexible (Stevens 1995). During this period, all schools were required to reconceptualise and reconstruct their curricula, a process which we explore in more detail later in this book and which many practitioners have come to see as productive and valuable in itself (Byers and Rose 1996; Carpenter and Ashdown 1996). Further, many practitioners previously hostile to the notion of a National Curriculum have become ardent advocates of the principle of entitlement to breadth and balance and resist tendencies to move back towards more narrow, utilitarian models of the curriculum based on notions about relevance (Byers 1999).

In the course of this debate about a curriculum for all, then, perceptions about the curriculum have certainly changed. We would argue that ideas about schools and learners have altered too. Arguably, special schools have become, in the perceptions of colleagues in the mainstream of education and in the minds of parents and pupils, less 'special' and more like other schools. The curriculum framework and some of the language used in discourse about school structures, teaching, learning and pupil progress are now common to all. There is less focus upon the differences between mainstream schools and the special sector and more tendency to accept similarities. In the same way, pupils with learning difficulties, for example, are less likely to be regarded as requiring a different curriculum and special ways of working. In establishing routes to access and achievement for these pupils within a shared curriculum, practitioners have found themselves challenging the very definitions of concepts of 'learning difficulty' or 'special educational need'.

What are we to learn ourselves from these events? It may be interesting to reflect upon some of the responses to SCAA's (1996) publication exploring the possibility of pupils with profound and multiple learning difficulties making progress and showing achievement within the National Curriculum. Some commentators hold that certain groups of pupils within specialist environments cannot participate meaningfully in a full range of experiences and activities, even when there is evidence to the contrary. We would rather suggest that established definitions of these pupils, their schools and the learning that they do are uncertain and problematic.

Revitalised practices

Sebba and Ainscow (1996) would agree that colleagues in the mainstream and special sectors of education need to re-evaluate their views of schooling, of the curriculum and of learners. They propose that inclusion is not simply about relocating learners into shared buildings. It is also, in their terms, about innovation, experimentation and about professional risk taking. They suggest that schools which are committed to the process of becoming more inclusive will develop problem solving cultures of the kind that we mean to illustrate in this book. They will foster working practices based on joint planning, teacher partnerships and critical friendships. This collaborative staffroom culture will support practice in classrooms where cooperation and peer coaching within mixed groups of pupils is fostered so that there is active and meaningful participation for all learners (Smith 1998). Sebba and Ainscow further argue that inclusive classroom practices will make use of a varied, flexible and diverse range of teaching methods and acknowledge and be responsive to the reactions and perceptions of the pupils themselves. In short, then, the process of including pupils with learning difficulties must focus on *how* teaching and learning is done as well as on *where* pupils are taught.

Other commentators echo the key themes of Sebba and Ainscow's analysis. Thomas *et al.* (1998) in their study of inclusion note, for example, that it is important to provide frequent opportunities for members of staff to plan together, in good quality non-contact time, in order to undertake the radical review of the curriculum; the ongoing integration of pupils' individual programmes into whole class lessons; and the day by day differentiation which, in their view, helps to make the inclusive classroom effective for all learners.

It is interesting to observe that arguments in favour of inclusive practice now focus on educational progress, achievement and quality of learning rather than solely upon equity and equality of opportunity. Sebba and Sachdev (1997), in their review of international research, point out that pupils with learning difficulties have much to gain educationally from inclusive practices, perhaps most particularly in terms of language, reading, skills for learning and skills for living. Sebba and Sachdev also emphasise that other pupils achieve 'as well or better standards' and make 'the same or more progress' in inclusive classrooms as in traditional mainstream classes. In making a success of inclusive practices, Sebba and Sachdev again stress the importance of shared planning, focusing increasingly on issues of teaching and learning, and emphasise that staff will need to be supported in learning to work together in new ways. They note that one of the critical factors in the success of this shared planning, and in the success of inclusive initiatives, is the provision of a wide variety of teaching methods.

The role of the special school and the specialist teacher

If it is true that the development of a more inclusive education system entails the promotion of enhanced educational opportunities, with meaningful involvement in classroom activity and full participation in the curriculum ensured for all learners, then special schools and specialist teachers can begin to see themselves as having a valuable role to play in the inclusion process. Some of the key themes and practices that we have brought into our work for this project, for example, are:

- that opportunities for good quality planning between staff in and across classroom and departmental teams should be provided;
- that this shared planning should be facilitated and shaped by focused support;
- that the curriculum should be planned, reviewed and prepared for implementation through cooperative endeavour;
- that discussion between staff should focus on the detail of planning for teaching and learning, with an emphasis on providing a range of teaching methods;
- that staff should acknowledge and take account of the responses of pupils in reviewing and adapting their approaches to teaching.

We maintain that these are all aspects of inclusive practice which can be fostered within specialist provision as well as in the mainstream. Indeed, we would suggest that the expertise that has developed in special schools over recent years gives specialist colleagues an important opportunity to contribute to the development of increasingly inclusive policies and practices.

In this sense, it is encouraging to note the position which is adopted in Chapter 3 of *A Programme of Action* (DfEE 1998a). Here it is argued that the evolution of an 'increasingly inclusive education system' will entail developing the role of the special school and 'promoting special schools' contribution'. In the *Programme of Action*, inclusion is envisioned as 'a process, not a fixed state', and as encompassing, in addition to the idea of pupils with learning difficulties being placed, full time, in mainstream schools, a range of possibilities which includes:

- all pupils being enabled to participate 'in the curriculum and social life of mainstream schools' – perhaps for part of the week, the term or their school career;
- all pupils being enabled to participate in learning which 'leads to the highest possible level of achievement';
- all pupils being equipped to participate 'in the full range of social experiences and opportunities once they have left school'.

These are possibilities which we see as being realistic and optimistic and which suggest that that there may be diversity of practice within an inclusive framework. That diversity may, in turn, encompass aims towards which staff in special schools can make positive contributions alongside, or in partnership with, their mainstream colleagues. The *Programme of Action* goes on to suggest some of the ways in which these aims may be achieved. It is made clear that 'specialist provision – often, but not always in special schools – will continue to play a vital role' but special schools should:

- cultivate and facilitate 'close links with neighbouring mainstream schools';
- become 'much more closely integrated into local patterns of provision' by working with mainstream schools and exploring the possibility of sharing responsibility for pupils;
- become 'confident, outward-looking centres of excellence' by building on 'their strengths' in order to become 'an integral part of an inclusive education system for children in their area'.

In writing this book, we declare an interest in attempting to meet these challenges. We wish to present a view of inclusion written from the perspective of those whose background is in special schools. We contend that a critical awareness of the strengths and shortcomings of specialist provision should inform the process of developing, in the *Programme of Action*'s phrase, 'an increasingly inclusive education system'.

This will be crucial if, as the *Programme of Action* proposes, staff in special and mainstream schools are to 'work more closely together to maximise inclusion' with staff in special schools developing roles as sources of 'expertise, advice and professional development for mainstream colleagues'. For many teachers working in special schools, the idea of sharing the intricacies of their classroom practices with colleagues in the mainstream will be challenging. There will be some uncertainty about whether any pedagogical expertise truly exists in special schools. There will be a crisis of confidence as the prospect of becoming sources of advice and guidance looms. There will be a need to develop clarity about:

- the nature and extent of the significant body of knowledge or expertise that exists in special schools;
- the procedures, practices, methods or attitudes that characterise the work of specialist staff;
- the most effective ways of ensuring an exchange of views between colleagues in mainstream and special schools so that it is mutually supportive and to the benefit of all pupils, including those with learning difficulties.

This book attempts to contribute to the process of developing that clarity.

In summary

We have used this section in order to review the development of the idea of including those pupils who are currently referred to as having 'learning difficulties'. This process has entailed a series of changes of approach in the education of these pupils. We now suggest that practitioners and policy makers need to think about more than simply the location of pupils in mainstream or special schools. The significant characteristics of inclusive classrooms which we have acknowledged in our work include:

- fostering an attitude which welcomes all pupils, values their diversity and actively seeks to maintain them as class members;
- responding to pupil diversity by restructuring elements like staffing arrangements, the physical environment, the curriculum and teaching and learning processes;
- maintaining a commitment to innovation, experimentation, problem solving and professional risk taking;

- developing shared planning and working practices involving collaborative partnerships and critical friendships between different members of the staff team;
- promoting cooperative ways of working, peer support and interdependence among mixed groups of pupils in the classroom;
- using a wide and varied range of teaching methods in order to:
  - facilitate meaningful involvement and the fullest possible participation for all pupils;
  - accommodate and promote diversity in experience, in learning preferences and in skills and strategies for learning among individual pupils.

We have argued that these ways of working may, as we move towards a more inclusive system of education, characterise classrooms in special as well as mainstream schools. Indeed, we assert that special schools, and certainly specialist staff, will have a crucial contribution to make to the debate about policy and practice as the inclusion process gathers pace. We have also noted the ways in which policy and practice have moved away from stark divisions between 'normal' and 'subnormal' or 'mainstream' and 'special' towards more complex views of the differences and similarities between various learners and the approaches which have evolved in attempts to meet their educational needs. In the next section, we explore these ideas in greater depth and look at what is entailed, for teachers and learners, in evolving practices, changing classrooms and developing schools.

3 Descriptions

In this section, we address three key questions:

- What is involved in different types of teaching for teachers?
- What are the necessary conditions for change: flexible teachers – flexible learners?
- What is involved in different types of teaching for learners?

In responding to these questions, we trace the history of the debate about teaching methods in special schools; describe the process of supporting staff in their short term planning; and provide analyses of the learning requirements imposed upon pupils by a range of teaching methods.

What is involved in different types of teaching for teachers?

This is not a book which is centrally about access to the content of the curriculum. We regard that as a debate which has largely been resolved (see below). For the purposes of our discussion, the curriculum may be seen as a vehicle for teaching and learning and, at least in part, for enabling pupils to see themselves as effective learners, and to develop an awareness of their learning preferences which will remain relevant in the world beyond school.

Staff working with pupils with learning difficulties, we suggest, have a significant contribution to make to the pursuit of these outcomes and we begin our analysis of this potential by looking at practice in special schools.

Methods in special schools: objectives based approaches and organisational strategies

As we have seen, special schooling for pupils with severe and profound and multiple learning difficulties has its origins back in the 1970s. In those early days, teachers in the newly-founded special schools were encouraged to teach using what became known as the objectives based approach. Without engaging here in the detail of a debate which is recorded elsewhere (see, for example, Sebba *et al.* 1993; Byers 1994a; Collis and Lacey 1996), it might be worth providing a brief summary of the characteristics, from the teacher perspective, of this way of working. Objectives based approaches used in special schools in the 1970s and 1980s tended to emphasise:

- individual tuition, with a sense that one-to-one teaching represented the ideal learning situation;
- the setting of precise, observable, measurable, behaviourally quantifiable objectives for each learner;

- step by step learning programmes, with formal task analysis used in order to identify the sub-skills which would gradually build into whole new skills;
- a carefully structured approach to the teaching of specific skills using techniques like backward or forward chaining or shaping;
- tight control of setting conditions and adult prompts;
- the establishment of rigorous success criteria;
- frequent and detailed recording, testing, assessment and re-assessment;
- the extensive use of extrinsic rewards and reinforcers such as food, tokens or praise.

This sort of approach was formalised in a range of detailed teaching programmes, for example, EDY (Foxen and McBrien 1981) and Portage (White and Cameron 1986), which were adopted by many special schools. These materials were often founded upon an analysis of the development of very young, non-disabled children and were then brought into use in all-age schools for pupils with severe or profound and multiple learning difficulties. These sorts of programmes continue to have their uses, their advantages and their adherents (see, for example, Farrell *et al.* 1992) but also, from the late 1980s on, attracted a growing criticism (see, for example, Billinge 1988).

Over time, the range of methods designed or adapted for use in special education has been extended. Some of these methods maintain ideological consistency with the objectives based way of working. For example, the TEACCH approach (Landrus and Mesibov undated), designed for use with pupils on the autistic spectrum, draws recognisably upon the behaviourist tradition. It is an approach which is heavily structured, relying on precise and detailed teacher direction and 'scheduling'. Pupils in a TEACCH classroom tend to work individually and even in isolation from one another. Again, some approaches to the management of pupils' problematic behaviours continue to emphasise many of the aspects of behaviourism. Zarkowska and Clements' (1994) STAR approach, for example, is essentially an elaboration of the antecedents-behaviour-consequences formula promulgated within the behaviourist tradition.

Some formulae which have been proposed for use by staff in specialist contexts prove, on examination, to be organisational strategies rather than teaching methods. More detail about these sorts of approaches to organisational issues, and about the ways in which they can be mixed and matched, is provided in Ouvry (1987) and Ware (1994). We would suggest that staff in specialist contexts have learned a great deal about interdependence and collaboration across the various disciplines represented in a staff team from exploring and experimenting with organisational strategies like these.

Methods in special schools: negotiated learning and interactive approaches

Other approaches used in specialist contexts have evolved from ideological positions which contrast significantly with the behaviourist paradigm. The High/Scope approach, for example, (High/Scope Press 1991) was originally designed for use with young children in nursery or day care situations but has been adapted and adopted for use with pupils with learning difficulties. In

High/Scope, the emphasis is on the learner's own motivations, initiations and interests. The principles underpinning this way of working include:

- making a wide variety of interesting materials and resources freely accessible and available to learners;
- encouraging pupils to handle and explore materials at will;
- encouraging pupils to choose preferred activities and select their own materials and resources;
- valuing all the communicative attempts made by learners;
- using adults as supporters, facilitators or partners sharing in the pupil's chosen activity – the task for the adult here is to allow the pupil to take the initiative and then to guide the learner through 'key experiences' and towards new skills.

The key structural template in a High/Scope session encompasses three phases, usually characterised as plan-do-review. Staff and pupils first spend time together planning the activities in which the pupil means to engage. During this phase, the pupil considers a range of options and discusses them with staff and with other learners. In this way, pupils develop a sense of themselves as choice makers and as agents of control and begin to anticipate forthcoming activities. During the work-focused phase of the session, pupils implement their plans. The adults' role during this period is to observe, share and participate in activities. The aim is to encourage and extend the learners' experiences but not to direct them. At the end of a typical High/Scope activity session, pupils and staff come together in order to recall and review their experiences and compare these to their original plans. In this phase, staff may support learners in presenting their ideas to their peers.

Contrasting with behaviourist approaches in similar ways, Intensive Interaction (Nind and Hewett 1994) and other interactive approaches (Smith 1987; Coupe O'Kane and Smith 1994; Collis and Lacey 1996) focus on:

- pupil initiation and an active role for the learner;
- partnership and negotiation between teacher and learner;
- control within the learning situation shared between teacher and learner;
- an absence of teacher-imposed, pre-defined targets or objectives.

Indeed Intensive Interaction (which was originally based on observations of infant–caregiver interactions and was then developed as a way of working in residential settings with young people and adults with profound learning difficulties, difficulties with communication and often very problematic behaviours) is characterised by its originators as 'taskless'. Intensive Interaction is now widely used in special schools, often provided as part of the taught day alongside more formal lessons focusing on National Curriculum subjects. In addition to the principles noted above, Intensive Interaction's advocates emphasise the learner's right to call a halt to or to withdraw from activities, and the avoidance of compulsion, explicitly in order to counteract what Nind and Hewett saw as teacher dominance and rigidity of control within the behaviourist tradition.

By the latter part of the 1980s, then, staff in specialist contexts (and their pupils) were already dealing with a dichotomy between these contrasting models. For some, this resulted in confusion. For those loyal to a particular cause, there was an opportunity for lively and partisan debate. This debate rolls on. In 1992, Farrell undertook a detailed defence of behavioural teaching in which he sought to counter many of the arguments of behaviourism's critics. He also made a number of points which are relevant to this chapter – for example, that the behavioural approach is not suited to all areas of learning; that pupils need group experiences as well as one-to-one teaching; that learning should, where possible, take place in contexts meaningful to the learner.

These sorts of points were elaborated by others (see, for example, Rose 1991; Sebba *et al.* 1993; Byers 1994b) but Farrell (1992), and later Kessissoglou and Farrell (1995), also introduced the intriguing notion that behavioural and interactive approaches could be used successfully alongside one another and even interwoven within the same session. For the pragmatic and worldly-wise, this may appear to offer a middle way in which the best aspects of contrasting traditions can be put to use in the classroom for different purposes. While this idea may have its attractions, we would suggest that it is not entirely unproblematic and that there are significant challenges, for teachers and learners, entailed in changing pedagogical gear, as it were, during sessions, during the day or even at various points in the week's timetable. We are, however, not interested in pursuing a dualistic, either–or debate about the relative merits of contrasting approaches. We intend, rather, to take this debate towards a balanced view of a range of approaches and a celebration of diversity, eclecticism and plurality within the classroom.

Methods in special schools: the introduction of the National Curriculum

The first version of the National Curriculum was delivered into the midst of this situation. It was championed as a curriculum for all (NCC 1989) and as providing a unitary model for education through the compulsory years of schooling which would include pupils with learning difficulties. In 1992, National Curriculum Council published *Curriculum Guidance 9*. This document (NCC 1992) contained relatively few references to teaching methods. The major issue then and for some time to come (see, for example MEC Teacher Fellows 1990; Ashdown *et al.* 1991; Carpenter *et al.* 1996) was mostly about the practicability of creating meaningful access, for pupils with learning difficulties, to the content of the National Curriculum. The guidance explored the idea of addressing 'individual skills, needs and interests' within group activity focused on the National Curriculum (see also Byers 1990), but this concerned traditional objectives rather than learning style preferences. The guidance did mention the need for staff to ask themselves whether they provided 'sufficient variety in the methods used to teach reading' as one example in a list of possible issues meriting audit and review. It also provided a brief discussion of group work and the idea of 'jigsawing' roles or tasks for individual pupils within a group activity (see also Rose 1991).

But concerns about curriculum content were not supposed to overwhelm healthy debate about teaching methods. National Curriculum Council (NCC 1990) was at pains to delineate the breadth of the whole curriculum and to celebrate the flexibilities which teachers were meant to explore within the National Curriculum framework:

> The Education Reform Act does not prescribe how pupils should be taught. It is the birthright of the teaching profession, and must always remain so, to decide on the best and most appropriate means of imparting education to pupils. If the whole curriculum is to mean anything then it must be imparted by use of a wide range of teaching methods, formal and informal, class and group, didactic and practical. The wide range of skills which pupils must acquire must be reflected in an equally wide variety of approaches to teaching. (p. 7)

The introduction of the National Curriculum into special schools certainly did involve a review of teaching methods. It became apparent that a full and honest implementation of the programmes of study for many specific subjects would entail some consideration of issues like pupil-led initiation, exploration, investigation and problem solving (Fagg and Skelton 1990; Mount and Ackerman 1991). Sebba (1994), in her analysis of matters that should be set out within a scheme of work implementing history for pupils with learning difficulties, includes the need to specify 'methods – teaching approaches to be used, pupil grouping etc.' Staff in special schools were therefore encouraged to think about providing variety in their choice of teaching methods.

Methods in special schools: other influences

Some commentators began to make links between this analysis and the debate, outlined above, concerning the ideological contrasts between the various methods and approaches which had been in use in special schools. Further, there were some suggestions that the increased range of teaching methods with which special schools had been encouraged to experiment in engaging with the introduction of the National Curriculum was itself likely to promote positive progress towards autonomy and empowerment in pupils with learning difficulties (see Sebba *et al.* 1993; Byers 1994a; and Byers 1994b). Put simply, the idea was that the increase in pupil-directed learning brought about by the introduction of the National Curriculum in special schools counteracted the overemphasis on teacher prescription (and the resulting increase in pupil dependence) entailed in the long-term use of behavioural methods.

The introduction of the records of achievement model at around the same time had a similar impact. Authors like Lawson (1992) or Hardwick and Rushton (1994) noted that the proposed negotiation of targets, pupil self recording and pupil ownership of records produced classroom processes in which there was an increase in the levels and the quality of pupil control. Arguably, the full implementation of the *Code of Practice* (DfE 1994) according to its stated principles would also have had a major influence upon issues of pupil control, but the *Code* was not perceived at the time as having real significance for practice in special schools (Lewis *et al.* 1996). It is worthy of note, however, that although practices and procedures were neither well-established nor widespread, some special educators appeared to be at the leading edge of developments in this area (Tilstone 1991c; Smith 1994; Carpenter and Ashdown 1996).

The clamour about the sense of overload which many schools were experiencing as a result of attempting to implement the full content of the National Curriculum led to review (Dearing 1993). Although most of the problems with the implementation of the National Curriculum at the time related to an excess of content, the Dearing review teams, in attempts to create a leaner, fitter, more flexible curriculum, stripped many of the references to teaching methods out of the programmes of study (Byers 1994c). As Byers and Rose (1996) note, these methods had, for pupils with learning difficulties, 'brought another perspective regarding balance and variety to the classroom'. It became important to ensure that there was no return to the previous narrow range of approaches to teaching. As this debate continues, many commentators encourage specialist teachers to ensure that the spectrum of methods brought into special schools along with the subjects of the National Curriculum continues to expand and proliferate.

The introduction of OFSTED's (1995) *Guidance on the Inspection of Special Schools* extended this debate. According to OFSTED:

> The choice of teaching methods and organisational strategies is a matter for the school and the teacher's discretion. This should be based on the objectives of the lesson and factors such as the number of pupils, their age, attainment and behaviour, and the nature of the resources and accommodation. (p. 71)

OFSTED's guidance goes on to suggest examples of teaching methods that might be used in special schools and to emphasise again that there might be a complex relationship between teacher preference, the demands of the curriculum and pupils' individual needs:

> Teaching methods include exposition, explanation, demonstration, discussion, practical activity, investigation, testing and problem-solving. The test of their effectiveness is the extent to which they extend or deepen pupils' knowledge and understanding and develop their skills. They are likely to do so when they are selected and handled with careful regard to:
>
> - the nature of the curricular objectives being pursued; and
> - what pupils know, understand and can do, and what they need to learn next.
>
> (p. 72)

The guidance suggests that there might be similar decisions to be made about options in classroom organisation. The decisions that teachers are encouraged to make here may involve pupil grouping, for example:

> Key issues with regard to how pupils are organised in the class are:
>
> - whether the objectives are best achieved by pupils working alone, in pairs or small groups, or all together;
> - whether the form of organisation allows the teacher to interact with pupils positively and economically.
>
> Good teaching will employ different organisational strategies to pursue different curricular objectives. (p. 72)

The OFSTED guidance also has comments to make about the skills of the teacher in promoting pupil involvement and in managing the roles of various members of the classroom staff team:

> In relation to whole-class teaching inspectors should consider how well the teacher manages explanation, questioning and discussion so that all pupils are involved and stimulated. In observing group and individual work inspectors should look at how the teacher interacts with pupils to keep the work focused and moving at pace. Inspectors should identify whether the teacher is using his or her teaching skills rather than merely servicing the tasks. This is particularly an issue when classroom activities cover a number of subjects and use a wide range of resources, including other adults. (p. 72)

Short term planning: prescription and professional judgement

We have reproduced these extracts here in some detail because they contribute significantly to the debate that we wish to have about the importance of making such decisions conscious and subjecting them to review and evaluation along with subject policies and schemes of work. In response to OFSTED's call for pedagogical variety in special school classrooms, we have encouraged staff with whom we have worked to list the range of methods which they might use in their practice. Ideas generated as outcomes of this task include:

discussion   problem solving   experimentation   role play   exploration
chalk and talk   demonstration   explanation   information giving   investigation
collaboration   modelling   practical activity   circle time

Colleagues have suggested that they use a variety of resources in order to stimulate pupils' learning, including:

speech   text   pictures   video   graphics   symbols   computers
audio-visual aids   real objects   multi-sensory environments
the outdoor environment   the community

and that pupils may be organised in groupings of various sizes for a range of purposes:

whole school   whole department   whole class
group   small group   sets   pairs   one-to-one.

While OFSTED (1995) exhorts teachers to make informed and focused decisions about these aspects of practice, however, other initiatives have been less permissive. The National Strategies, for example, for Literacy and Numeracy (DfEE 1998b; 1998c; and 1999) define for staff, in detail, strategies for classroom organisation, pupil groupings, use of resources and teaching methods which are recommended in pursuit of raised standards in the key areas of literacy and numeracy. Once again, the introduction of these initiatives into special schools appears to have had the effect of revitalising practice, although concerns have been raised (Byers 1999) about their impact upon breadth and balance in the curriculum and about the appropriateness of the proposed content and methods for some pupils, for example, those with profound and multiple learning difficulties.

In effect, these initiatives bring a significant measure of prescription into an area in which staff have previously been encouraged to exercise their professional judgement as part of the 'birthright of the teaching profession' (NCC 1990). We are proposing that staff need to be reflective about these processes in order to promote participation and inclusion for pupils with learning difficulties in classroom activity. We further suggest that this constitutes an integral part of that phase of the curriculum implementation process which is generally referred to as short term planning (see, for example, SCAA 1995; SCAA 1996; Byers and Rose 1996). SCAA (1995) says that short term planning is 'usually carried out individually by class teachers' and that it focuses on 'day to day teaching and assessment'. We propose (with acknowledgements to SCAA 1996 and Byers and

Rose 1996) that short term planning for pupils with learning difficulties will focus on:

- differentiating schemes of work in order to promote access and participation for a range of pupils;
- integrating targets from pupils' individual education plans, which may be set in terms of cross-curricular or key skills, into subject focused teaching;
- selecting and using environments, equipment and resources effectively with due regard to lesson content and pupil need;
- deploying staff in support of pupil learning;
- grouping pupils in a variety of ways;
- creating opportunities to record and assess pupils' progress and achievement in relation to individual targets and subject aims;
- developing balance and variety across a range of teaching methods and learning styles.

We therefore argue, with Lewis (1992), that the process of making decisions about teaching methods should be regarded as part of the task of differentiating schemes of work for pupils with learning difficulties through short term planning. As we have seen, some methods have evolved or have been designed for use with pupils at certain age stages. Staff who work with pupils with learning difficulties often find, however, that methods which originate in work with younger pupils (such as discovery learning, circle time or the High/Scope method) continue to be relevant and appropriate for some older learners. Other methods which have traditionally been used in the mainstream of education with older pupils (such as exposition at the blackboard, questioning and discussion or testing hypotheses) may appear to be problematic for some pupils with learning difficulties. At the same time, as we have suggested above, some methods are closely associated with certain subject areas (problem solving in design and technology, for example, or investigation in science) yet staff working with pupils with learning difficulties have found it profitable to extend their use of these methods into work in other areas of the curriculum in order to make learning more available to pupils who find less active methods inaccessible. Whether decisions about pedagogy are to be imposed upon classroom practice or made in the light of informed professional judgement, the debate about teaching methods for pupils with learning difficulties is therefore now more open and potentially more productive than it has ever been.

In summary

This section has reviewed the development of teaching methods in special schools. We have noted the impact that this process has had upon staff, suggesting that some changes in practice have entailed a paradigm shift, for example, from teacher prescribed behavioural methods; through interactive ways of working in which all aspects of practice are open to negotiation with pupils; to broad approaches and detailed techniques which are imposed from central sources. Throughout this process of change and adaptation, we suggest, staff in special schools have learned to become more flexible and, in particular, to challenge and alter their perceptions about what it is possible for pupils with learning difficulties to do and to achieve. In this way, we suggest, staff in special schools have, in the sorts of ways that we have proposed in previous sections:

- learned to embrace and value uncertainty;
- challenged, changed and, in many cases, abandoned their preconceptions about:
  - pupils with learning difficulties and the teaching methods with which they are able to engage meaningfully;
  - curriculum content and the teaching methods which are associated with certain subjects and pupils in certain age groups;
- become more effective by becoming more reflective as practitioners;
- developed a curriculum which:
  - is broad, balanced and relevant;
  - is diverse in content, in method and in outcome;
  - meets the individual needs of pupils with learning difficulties.

We do not suggest, however, that this position has been arrived at without struggle. Indeed, staff who work with pupils with learning difficulties continue to look for support in engaging with the complexities of short term planning. In the following paragraphs and in the next section of this book, we describe some of the reflective processes with which staff have engaged in order to try to come to understandings about what is entailed in making aspects of the curriculum and a range of teaching methods available to pupils with learning difficulties.

What are the necessary conditions for change: flexible teachers – flexible learners?

It is recognised that typical school structures and traditional curriculum demarcation militates against teacher collaboration and contributes towards the resulting characteristic feature of 'loose-coupling' as termed by Skrtic (1991). We suggest that promoting and articulating a whole-school commitment to meeting the individual needs of all pupils, regardless of ability, transcends organisational and curriculum arrangements and indeed exerts internal pressure for change upon school structures. A direct and practical commitment to meeting individual needs causes radical reappraisal of the form and content of staff development giving rise to what Garner *et al.* (1995) refer to as the 'new paradigm of learning'. Creative and opportunistic staff training arrangements will serve as a medium of organisational change by way of what can be usefully described as re-designing the work place through the work-shop (Joyce 1992).

A common aim for all

A serious and concerted intention to meet the needs of all, including those with learning difficulties, provides the necessary conditions for ensuring that all teachers, regardless of background, have equal value in the process of school based curriculum and staff development – all have something to learn as well as something to contribute towards professional dialogue. This inclusiveness also allows the curriculum, regardless of subject status, to be used as a vehicle for meeting individual pupil priority areas of learning – the curriculum, therefore, becomes the medium through which we both teach and learn and, as such, becomes more needs led than purely subject or syllabus driven.

The central challenge within a culture of collaborative improvement is to bring about a genuine team approach towards meeting the needs of all, while not compromising professional or individual teacher autonomy. This can be facilitated by a clearly articulated common motivation: the desire to improve the overall learning of pupils. In order to improve the learning of all pupils, the whole curriculum must be responsive. The curriculum must become highly differentiated in order to respond to the needs of all individuals, regardless of background. However, as O'Brien (1998) states, 'the differentiated curriculum cannot depend solely on the intuitive or charismatic teacher. Differentiation has to be grounded in principles that inform teaching style and ensure curriculum responsivity.'

Teachers must be responsive and flexible in order to draw on a wide repertoire of teaching practices to enable them to match a particular aspect of curriculum content to the distinct needs of a group of pupils. In order for teachers to become 'flexible teachers' they must themselves become 'flexible learners'. O'Brien continues, 'the collaborative nature of a differentiated learning environment must not be overlooked – the children can learn with each other and from each other, and the learning network increases when teachers are added to this interactive partnership.'

A responsive curriculum will be adaptable in terms of content, that is, it will be differentiated. Serious regard, however, needs to be given to the teaching approach, methods and styles adopted by the teacher if the curriculum is to be translated, conveyed and rendered accessible to all. This is a challenge for all involved in teaching, and certainly proves an even greater challenge in the mainstream secondary school where subject division is marked and where particular teaching approaches are often associated with specific subjects. As Garner *et al.* (1995) state, 'subject teachers are often said, even by themselves, to be teaching geography (or whatever) not children.' The underlying assumption is that readying the children to 'receive' geography is the function of some other teacher . . . and that the special needs support teacher's role is to carry this out for the 'stragglers' who are not ready for the absorption of the subject knowledge.

Within such a stratified environment, particular pupils will inevitably be excluded from certain areas of the curriculum if their own learning style does not match with the predominant teaching approach inherent within a given subject. This is a further imperative reinforcing the need for teachers to talk openly to each other about their teaching within and across the whole curriculum and about what works for them in particular contexts and with particular pupils.

Creating conditions for focused reflection

Quality time must be found within the busy school routine for teacher reflection and discussion of teaching and learning. One of the phase facilitators at St John's School said, 'it's a meeting time when people are expected to be there so we sit down and do it. If I said "could we all sit down for an hour and talk" there would not be the same response so meeting times had to be made and that has been very useful.' A radical re-appraisal of the allocation of non-contact time and a practical analysis of the manner in which time is used is required in order to maximise efficiency and effectiveness of focused reflection. Exchanges will take place within both formal and informal settings and will range from structured debate to open-ended dialogue. Examples of such time allocation may include training days, regular phase curriculum meetings, specific 'teacher support team' meetings, 'peer coaching' planning and feedback meetings, impromptu end of day class team talk. The two common underlying features to all sessions are:

- content is that of teaching and learning within the context of the school curriculum;
- delivery is very much 'on the job' providing tangible links between theory and practice.

Dialogue within these planned and incidental meetings will have observable and ongoing impact upon the quality of learning for pupils. Whilst possessing certain essential features, such regular quality time built into the school infrastructure assists in developing what we describe as 'the cycle of collaborative development' (see Figure 3.1), and is indicative of a culture of continuous improvement. The essential features seen as critical reflect the 'key training components' as identified by Joyce and Showers (1988):

- presentation of theory or description of skill or strategy;
- modelling or demonstration of skills or models of teaching;
- practice in simulated and classroom settings;
- structured and open-ended feedback;
- coaching for application. (pp. 68/69)

The continuous cycle of collaborative development is facilitated by the structures and processes at work within the school. The group or team is an essential element within this process. One practical strategy, which may be employed by a group to raise awareness and cause reflection on teaching and learning, is the development of a script or structured discussion plan. Such a strategy is used at St John's School, the script generating a set of key questions, which are taken and discussed by teachers within a key-stage phase group. The rationale and format is discussed in Chapter 4. Discussion generated by such a strategic tool is focused, shared and ongoing over several meetings. Positive observable outcomes of this type of dialogue include amongst others enriched and consistent lesson planning; creative and consistent implementation of plans; and heavier investment in group processes.

In summary

This section has highlighted the key conditions necessary for the 'cycle of collaborative development' to emerge. These are:

- the articulation of a whole-school commitment to meet the needs of all pupils will generate the desire for change;
- all staff must be valued as having something to learn and offer in dialogue with others;
- the school curriculum must be needs led and not subject driven;
- strategic use must be made of 'meeting time' in order for staff to learn from each other.

Continuous Cycle of Collaborative Development

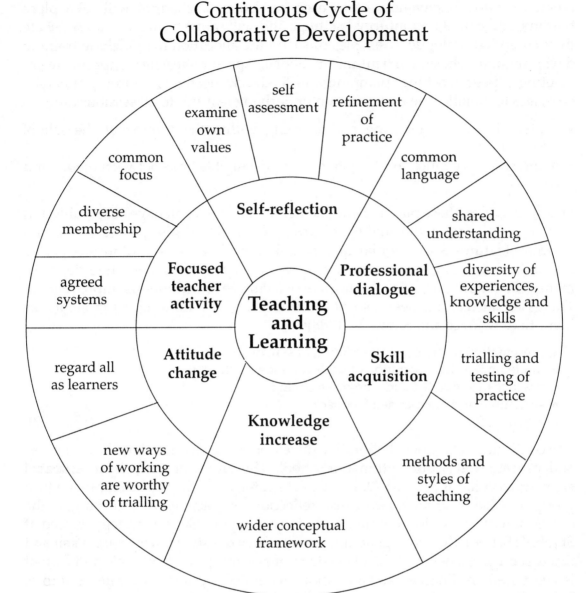

Figure 3.1 The cycle of collaborative development

What is involved in different types of teaching for learners?

Teachers use a range of approaches, techniques, methods and strategies that are influenced by personal style, situation, and pupil age, ability and attitude. We have already established within this book that neither teaching nor learning is completely dependent on style. Teachers need to adapt their teaching in order to meet the individual needs of all of the pupils in the class. This starts in the planning stages of converting long- and medium-term plans into short-term plans. At this stage the curriculum is differentiated in order to make it exciting, challenging and meaningful to all pupils. Riding and Rayner (1998) describe this process as being 'the integration of curriculum process and content, and more particularly, the individual learning style of students in the learning context'.

They describe the challenge for teachers as entailing the ability to differentiate the curriculum authentically, and conclude by highlighting the importance of meeting pupils' learning style needs, saying that it may: 'offer a way forward in teaching the hard to reach and reaching the hard to teach.'

Activities need to be planned that teach pupils the skills and strategies required to develop as individual human beings. The methods that the teacher chooses to implement the curriculum need to be pitched at the right level for each pupil, so that he can build on existing knowledge and understanding. In order to do this effectively the teacher needs to be able to present challenges appropriately for each pupil, and be clear that each pupil already has the necessary skills and knowledge to take his understanding one stage further. Activities may be planned that demand a level of thinking, but is it clear that all of the pupils have the capacity to work in that way at this stage in their development? Staff need to understand what skills and knowledge are required to work in a particular way, and what processes are entailed if the pupil is to gain the most from an activity that is taught by a particular method. By recognising and acknowledging these issues, teachers can address the teaching of the skills and knowledge that are necessary to equip the pupil with the flexibility to work in different ways.

Mulligan (1992) describes what he calls the seven internal processes for learning from experience as being the following:

- *willing* – which entails choosing, intending or being motivated to learn and the process of organising one's own learning;
- *remembering* – which can encompass learning through a range of modalities and includes, for example, sensory, symbolic, conceptual, verbal or physical memories;
- *reasoning* – which consists of responding to events by describing, interpreting, explaining or predicting;
- *feeling* – which involves making fluent emotional responses to the learning situation;
- *sensing* – which can incorporate first-hand experience gained through any or all of the available senses;
- *intuiting* – which entails being receptive, passive, attentive and listening to an internal voice as a starting point for enquiry or hypothesis;
- *imagining* – which involves conjuring up and trying out new ideas, actions, roles, behaviours and new, creative possibilities.

If a teacher is going to be truly successful in teaching pupils to learn from experience, then she has to be clear as to what preferences or styles and levels of skill a pupil has within each of a range of learning activities. Once she is clear on that, she then needs to support each pupil through the processes he finds difficult while encouraging him to be as independent as possible in carrying out those processes with which he is comfortable. Within that she needs to teach the pupil strategies for becoming more independent as a learner generally. When a pupil has understood and can utilise particular learning processes, then he can begin to make choices about the experience, make decisions about what parts of the experience to emphasise, and therefore make the experience a better one for himself. The task for the teacher is not simply providing a class with an 'experience'. Each experience will be a different one for each pupil, depending on what he brings to the lesson in terms of prior experiences, knowledge, understanding and skills. As Friere (1972) clearly suggests, the child is neither an empty 'receptacle' nor a 'docile listener'. For experience to have effect on learning, we have to try and understand how that experience impinges on each pupil. Kolb (1984) describes the process by which he believes this will be facilitated, saying that 'the education process begins by bringing out the learner's beliefs and values, examining them and testing them, and then integrating the new, more refined ideas into the person's belief systems.'

This process, which we explore in more detail in Chapter 4, demands a level of knowledge on the part of the teacher as to:

- how an individual pupil learns (his learning styles and preferences);
- his current level of understanding (the knowledge and skills that he brings to the lesson);
- his attitude towards learning in this particular context.

With this knowledge and understanding of the individual pupil, the teacher can attempt to clarify the new ideas, concepts and knowledge that she will be able to introduce in order to develop the learning process for each pupil. The understanding of dialogue between teachers and teachers, teachers and learners, and learners and the environment is vital in enabling the right questions to be asked in relation to learning from experience.

In devising the professional development activity which we describe below, we drew inspiration from Collis and Lacey (1996). These authors describe the empowering effect that becoming a problem solver can have upon pupils and argue that problem solving is an essential ingredient of everyday life as well as a key element in certain areas of the curriculum (Mount and Ackerman 1991). They go on to offer a succinct but illuminating analysis of what is entailed for learners in engaging with problem solving opportunities. We have used this analysis to great effect as an introduction to many professional development activities. Considering the internal processes involved in a teaching method which, on first encounter, appears to be essentially 'practical' in character has frequently been enlightening for staff.

Through collaborative reflection and discussion with staff from a range of educational settings we set out to analyse the processes that are entailed for learners within a range of teaching methods. The activity enabled staff to reflect upon and question their own teaching practices and highlight the gaps in pupil learning and experience that need to be filled in order for a pupil to make the most of the learning experiences on offer. The following are just examples, but we feel that the process of looking at teaching methods analytically and considering what is involved in these processes for learners is a valuable staff development opportunity in itself. It encourages reflection and dialogue, and supports the development of an understanding of the relationship between teaching and learning. By participating in this activity, we found that staff began to reflect on their use of the education terminology discussed earlier in this book, and were able to develop a shared understanding of what was meant by the methods and processes highlighted. We believe that staff benefited from being free to choose their own methods to break down into what they felt was entailed for the learner, rather than us being prescriptive in that experience. Exactly as we profess is important for the pupil, we as learners need our learning experiences to be relevant and meaningful to us. The following are therefore methods chosen by staff who were involved in the staff development activity described.

Processes involved in collaboration/group work

- *willing* – to be part of a group, to share effort, experience, knowledge and skills;
- *listening* – to other members of the group;
- *turn-taking/sharing* – within the group;
- *interacting* – within the group;
- *negotiating* – thoughts and ideas;
- *sensing* – other members of the group's individual needs;
- *knowing* – something from past experience that enables him to contribute to the activity;
- *accepting* – a role within the group;
- *focusing* – on the activity;
- *maintaining* – a goal;
- *supporting* – other members of the group;
- *recognising* – equality of status within the group;
- *contributing* – to the group;
- *evaluating* – the activity.

There are obvious prerequisite skills for working through collaboration and as a group, for example knowing that other people are there and having the skills and motivation to want to interact. The term 'group work' is used loosely in education, and pupils are sometimes described as doing 'group work' when in fact they are working within a group situation, in that they are physically positioned as a group, but are working individually. True 'group work' should involve actual interaction between all of the pupils present in the learning situation. As Stothard (1998) suggests when describing a 'group interaction' session, if the lesson is planned and presented appropriately, this can happen effectively for *all* pupils.

There are immense benefits for pupils through learning to work as a group and to collaborate. McNamara and Moreton (1997) describe the rationale for collaboration, saying that it helps learners to:

- develop their own thinking through talk;
- get support;
- value their achievements.

In order to recognise all learners as having opportunities for learning collaboratively, the first point could be amended to read 'develop their own thinking through communication'.

Group work and collaboration supports independent learning, and motivates the pupil to want to learn for himself. It can support the development of the pupils' confidence, which is necessary for future independent learning. As described in previous sections, one of the key goals of education and teaching is enabling pupils to learn for themselves, a skill that will carry them through life and not just through school.

Processes involved in problem solving/investigation

- *knowing* – there is a problem to solve;
- *willing* – to solve the problem;
- *analysing* – the task;
- *understanding* – the rules of the investigation;
- *asking* – appropriate questions;
- *answering* – questions;
- *choosing* – the right resources to use;
- *hypothesising* – about what might happen;
- *waiting* – for something to happen;
- *attending* – throughout the task;
- *sequencing* – thoughts and actions;
- *assessing* – results.

It was felt that within a group working on an investigative/problem solving activity, some pupils might be working on an experiential level, while others may be using more problem solving skills.

Pupils need to have acquired or have been taught the specific skills necessary for problem solving, and individual motivation is a key issue for the success of problem solving activities for specific pupils. Observations of pupil behaviour demonstrate that problem solving is possible if a pupil is determined to achieve what he has set out to achieve. A pupil may remember how he solved a similar problem before, and use that knowledge to support the way he behaves in this particular situation. The processes that occur during a problem solving activity may be spontaneous or strategically thought through. This could be explained by the idea of being aware or unaware of what you know or don't know. Teachers sometimes say that they don't know what they do, they just do it, and as learners we sometimes feel that we just 'know' things. However, if teachers can reflect on and encourage pupils to reflect on *how* they know *what* they know, then learners may be able to use that knowledge to support the development of knowing what they don't know they don't know. This idea is discussed further in Chapter 4. It is clear that the skills required in problem solving are important for the development of learning, and particularly independent learning.

Processes involved in exposition/explanation/discussion

- *listening* – to what is being said;
- *concentrating* – on the presentation;
- *answering* – questions;
- *allowing* – others to answer questions;
- *offering* – suggestions;
- *understanding* – that further investigations may be necessary;
- *knowing* – what can be achieved.

As we have found during the writing of this book, the process of discussion has enabled us to clarify, develop and refine our thinking and has been an essential ingredient to our learning process. In the same way supported discussion can help both adults and pupils to develop their learning skills and processes. Personal style and our ability to use strategies, as we have discussed previously in Chapter 2, affect learning. For many learners, discussion at whatever level is an important component in the development of understanding. Combined with more visual forms of presentation, discussion can bring alive a particular topic, and this interactive process can enable a learner to question and clarify thoughts and understanding. To maximise the benefits of discussion and interaction (through whatever means of communication) teachers need to support the pupils through the development of the processes listed above.

Processes involved in talk and chalk

- *knowing* – that talk is directed at them;
- *maintaining* – attention on the teacher;
- *listening* – to the information that is being imparted;
- *understanding* – language used;
- *processing* – information;
- *sequencing* – information;
- *retaining* – information;
- *relating* – to prior knowledge;
- *seeing* – the board;
- *understanding* – the organisation and content of written material;
- *tracking* – text;
- *understanding* – diagrams;
- *changing focus* – in line with the speed of the lesson, for example: the teacher changing from written to spoken information.

The success of this method of teaching relies on the skill of the teacher in presenting the materials in a way that is accessible to all pupils, and in organising the classroom, support staff and additional resources to ensure ease of participation for all. The visual and hearing abilities of the pupils need to be considered, and the presentation of the lesson will affect its success. There are obvious prerequisite skills for learning in this way, which are outlined above, and so knowledge of the pupils involved in the lesson will be required prior to planning. Staff within a professional development session we presented felt that if such a lesson was well planned and supported, and time was allocated to discuss individual pupils, differentiation could take place.

Processes involved in demonstration and imitation

- *sitting* – as part of a group;
- *focusing* – on the demonstration;
- *understanding* – the task that is being modelled;
- *looking* – at what is happening;
- *listening* – to what is being said;
- *understanding* – the communication methods being used;
- *processing* – the information;
- *recalling* – what has happened;
- *comparing* – with previous experience;
- *copying* – what has been demonstrated;
- *allowing* – someone to support you.

This method is reflected in White and Haring's (1980) hierarchy of skills which has been described in Chapter 2. Within this hierarchy the teacher will need to demonstrate what she wants the pupil to do, and then encourage and support the pupil to use this skill independently. As the pupil becomes more competent at demonstrating this skill, then the teacher will be able to withdraw some of her support. Solity (1988) suggests that this teaching method can be divided into procedures that illustrate the process a teacher would go through when using demonstration. The teacher would:

- model the skill;
- lead the pupil through the task at the same time;
- encourage the pupil to imitate the task;
- instruct the pupil through completing the task;
- test the pupil by asking him to complete the task.

Within this process the teacher may also cue, prompt, use fading, shaping or chaining. She will also feedback to the pupil, and in some cases use a reward as an extrinsic motivator.

Processes involved in individual work

- *accepting* – another person;
- *listening* – to what is being communicated;
- *focusing* – on the activity;
- *tolerating/accepting* – attention;
- *giving* – attention;
- *wanting* – to be there doing the activity.
- *understanding* – there is a beginning, middle and end to the activity;
- *becoming* – more independent;
- *using* – existing skills.

Individual work may occur within a group situation or as a one-to-one teaching activity. Some pupils may find the intensity of such a session pressurising, whereas other pupils will benefit from a learning situation that is free from distractions from other pupils and staff. There are obvious implications for this method of teaching in the structure of the environment and the staffing levels and organisation. There are also implications for future learning development for the pupil, and it is important to recognise that pupils need a balance of individual work and group activities so that they do not become reliant on constant adult interaction and intervention for their learning.

In summary

In this section, we have examined the process involved for learners in different methods of teaching. This discussion has highlighted the following points:

- the actual exercise of analysing teaching methods enables teachers to be clear about what is entailed in those methods for the learner;
- methods need to be chosen and pitched at the right level for individual learners in order for successful learning to take place;
- the information gained from reflecting on what is entailed for learners can be used to support the planning of future learning that is relevant and meaningful to the pupil;
- it is important for teachers to use a balance of selected teaching methods to give pupils a broad, balanced and variable range of learning experiences.

If readers wish to undertake similar analyses to those we have reported here, we provide, at Figure 3.2, a blank proforma which can be used in order to encourage staff, individually or in collaboration, to consider:

- When is a given teaching method most likely to be used, with whom, and to what purpose?
- Are there any particular organisational issues which arise from the use of this method?
- What is entailed for the teacher, in terms of techniques, skills, insights and strategies, in making this method work?
- Are there any particular issues about the sequence or structure of lessons which arise from the use of this method?
- What is entailed for pupils, in terms of the sorts of learning processes we have identified above, in being taught using this method?

We also provide, as Figure 3.3, a proforma which has explanatory prompts written into it. This sheet can be used as a handout in support of professional development sessions focusing on the analysis of teaching methods.

Many of the issues raised in this section are explored in more depth in the following pages.

Teaching method to be analysed:		
When . . . ?	With whom . . . ?	Why . . . is it used?
Organisational considerations:		
What is entailed for the teacher?		**What is entailed for the learner?**
Notes about structure:		

Figure 3.2 Proforma for analysis of teaching methods

Teaching method to be analysed: *What do you call this way of working?*

When . . . ? *Is there a time of day; a day of the week; a stage of the term; or a season of the year when this method works best?*	**With whom . . . ?** *Is this method best suited to certain groups of pupils, defined by age, interest or learning difficulty perhaps?*	**Why . . . is it used?** *Is this method particularly appropriate for teaching certain subjects or elements in the curriculum?*

Organisational considerations:
When using this method, is there an optimum group size; or a range of possibilities?
Is this method best suited to certain locations?
What resources, equipment, furnishings, room arrangements are required?
What levels of staff input are required to make this method safe? workable? successful?

What is entailed for the teacher? *Describe the techniques, skills, insights and strategies that the teacher will need to employ to make this method work.*	**What is entailed for the learner?** *Describe the experiences, learning activities, attitudes, concepts, understandings, skills, competencies and strategies presented to the learners in this method.*

Notes about structure:
Is there a particular sequence or order of events which you recommend for this method?
In what ways can this method be adapted to fit a variety of lesson structures?

Figure 3.3 Proforma with explanatory prompts

4 Developments

In this section, we address the following questions:

- How do teachers support learners and learning?
- How can pupils become self-aware and self-directing as learners?
- How can cultural change lead to improved practice?

In responding to these questions, we provide a means of analysing individual pupils' strengths, difficulties and preferences as learners; discuss the potential for making pupils more responsible for their own learning; and explore the extent to which schools can become self-determining and interdependent in seeking to promote more effective teaching and learning.

How do teachers support learners and learning?

Earlier in this book we discussed the power and value of collaborative reflection between teachers about learners and learning. The phase curriculum meetings outlined in Chapter 2 are one example of staff using quality time to reflect on the learners in their classes, and taking the opportunity to learn from each other's knowledge and experience. This time allows staff to develop their ideas together and supports not only the monitoring and evaluation of teaching and learning, but also the continuity and progression across the school. The following is a summary of the development of these meetings at St John's School.

Why were the phase curriculum meetings developed?

Subject coordinators had spent a lot of time developing schemes of work, and we needed to find a way of monitoring and evaluating their effectiveness within the classroom. We needed to see how the content of these documents could be transferred into the teaching and learning within the classroom and how the long and medium term plans related to short term plans and individual education plans. People were already collaborating in this process, but it was felt that if meeting time could be allocated for these discussions, then dialogue of a higher quality could take place. The school needs to recognise the power of such dialogue and put in place systems to support its development.

As has already been discussed, we felt that in order to develop and refine a culture of collaborative planning, monitoring and evaluation, we needed to introduce these meetings initially with a suggested *script sheet*. We offered staff the opportunity to use and develop it within phases, and bring suggested amendments back to the curriculum committee for discussion and agreement.

We did not want all of the phases to do something different as we felt that this would inhibit continuity and progression, an area highlighted in our post-OFSTED action plan and school development plan. However, the curriculum committee accepted all suggestions and a decision was made as to how the sheets would look. This has been and still is an evolutionary process, and as staff become more familiar with the process, the meeting will develop in line with the school's needs. The overall aim is that this type of discussion and collaborative planning, monitoring and evaluation will become so much a part of the culture of the school that the script will no longer be required, and the process will be automatic.

Staff are asked to make themselves familiar with all relevant curriculum documentation pertinent to the discussion, for example subject extension documents, prior to the meeting. Staff need to arrive at the meeting with relevant information on pupils' learning needs, profiles and other documentation, which will aid the planning process.

The following questions formed the original script, but these have since been amended in the light of phase discussion and experience.

What are the aims of the lesson?
How many lessons are needed to cover this unit of work? What will be the sequence of lessons – i.e. cumulative or free standing?
What are the objectives within the lessons?
What will be the content of the activities?
What teaching methods will be used?
How will we differentiate?
How can we structure each lesson to offer any of the following:

- problem-solving;
- choice making;
- peer interaction;
- IT supported learning?

What are the cross-curricular implications for these lessons?
What are the class/tutor grouping/integration implications for these lessons?
What assessment/recording opportunities/techniques should be created/available?
What specific resources will be required?
What do we need to do in terms of organising the physical environment?

After the meeting staff prepare short term plans which are copied and filed in the resource library. Also at the meeting an action plan is implemented which aims at work sharing and efficient use of teaching resources.

Perceived strengths

We would suggest that the following strengths have emerged from the phase curriculum meetings:

- Having allocated time for shared planning has strengthened the quality of discussion.
- Phases have been able to prepare resources for the following term's work in time for them to arrive for the start of a term.
- Staff have been able to share ideas and develop continuity and progression across the phase.
- Staff have been able to evaluate the medium term plans within the extension documents and check accessibility of content for all pupils.
- The process has enabled the school to share, refine and develop its thinking in relation to teaching, learning, monitoring and evaluation.
- The process has supported new staff in their induction into the school.
- The process has supported more long-standing members of staff in reflecting on and refining their own practice. It has made them aware of what they did not know they knew.
- It has given staff in Key Stages 3 and 4 and FE (Post 16) the opportunity to share information on students' cross-curricular skills in order to support their development in particular subjects.

Perceived difficulties

At the same time, the following difficulties have emerged:

- As this was a new process it has taken time for staff to become comfortable with this way of working.
- The differing number of staff in each phase has affected the type and quality of discussion that takes place.
- Early Years and Key Stage 1 are currently recognised as one phase which has meant that the type and detail of discussion has involved a wide range of ages as well as needs.
- Within Key Stages 3 and 4 some curriculum areas are taught by subject specialist teacher which has meant that the discussion has been more useful to particular members of staff in some instances.

Proposed future developments

In the light of these issues, we propose the following developments:

- The timing of these meetings is to be considered in the light of their varying success at different points in the term.
- The subject focus of these meetings is to be amended in the light of the monitoring and evaluation policy.
- The feasibility of separating Early Years from Key Stage 1 for all or part of these meetings is to be considered.
- Comments received from staff are to be discussed and used to improve the quality of these meetings.
- Balance and blend of staff is to be considered when planning staffing for the next academic year.

It was agreed that this process would be trialled for a year and then evaluated in the light of experience. As with many aspects of school development, it is vital that staff are encouraged to reflect on what worked or did not work, but in so doing also arrive at agreed realistic suggestions for the development of the use of this time in line with the original aims of developing processes for monitoring and evaluation, continuity and progression, and shared planning.

Examples of feedback and comments made on these meetings

Staff offered the following comments in response to the planned meetings:

- What gets written down is less important than the course you have to take.
- It's the face-to-face feedback, bouncing ideas off people, that has been very useful.
- It really informs you of future planning.
- It gives an opportunity to raise people's perceptions of learners.
- I think the most significant impact has been the collaborative planning – now we are actually sharing knowledge of students, knowledge of teaching and knowledge of curriculum.
- The amount of discussion has increased as the year has gone on and I think that the phase has also become much closer. Our discussion is quite open about most issues in school. I think there is quite a good level of trust amongst staff which I think is absolutely crucial.
- I think if we look back to a year ago we have moved on, but I think we need to move on further again.

Other examples of ways of promoting collaborative reflection include the use of lesson observations with feedback, and the use of video to analyse practice. Initially, the process of observation can feel very threatening for teachers, both as the person being observed and the person observing. Schools therefore need to consider and provide time for training on how to make observation a positive learning process for teachers, and a more comfortable experience for all. One phase facilitator said, 'we do get quite prickly about being observed, whether there is a reason or an ulterior motive. It would be nice to get to the stage where I'd feel comfortable with anyone coming into the classroom. The idea of observation would help to inform your own teaching and your own practice.' This idea reflects the notion of seeing ourselves as learners alongside our pupils.

The process of using classroom observations and analysis of video of our teaching can support this, and in our view has been successful within our own institution in giving staff the tools to develop teaching and learning effectively within the classroom. One of the phase facilitators at St John's School said, 'my most useful learning has been observation of other staff rather than just reading'. Figure 4.1 is an example of a video analysis sheet designed to help teachers to evaluate, reflect on, refine and develop their teaching practices.

Creating learning profiles

If staff are to be effective as teachers, they need to use their short term planning to reflect on their own roles. We suggest that they should also develop ways of considering the role of the learner in terms of individual strengths, difficulties and preferences.

The research on conditions such as Down's Syndrome (Wishart 1993) and Rett Syndrome (Lewis and Wilson 1996) tells us much about pupils' shared learning

---

Teacher: Jenny

Session: food technology (Key Stages 3 & 4)

1. What teaching approaches are you using in this session?
Verbal instruction
Physical demonstration

2. What particular methods or strategies are you employing within your teaching?
Questioning
Recall
Physical prompts
Verbal prompts
Problem solving
Demonstration and imitation

3. Are there any other teaching approaches, methods or strategies that you would consider using in this teaching situation that would support the development of the lesson?
Peer support – collaboration
More opportunities to learn through trial and error

4. What learning strategies are being used by pupils/students within this session?
Imitation
Trial and error
Problem solving

Figure 4.1 Analysis of video of teaching and learning

strengths and difficulties. The advice and suggestions outlined for pupils with particular conditions is immensely valuable in planning for teaching and supporting learning, and it would be foolish to ignore such information. Without rejecting the value of these findings about commonalities among certain groups of learners, we prefer to engage primarily with the notion that individual learners have individual patterns of learning characteristics. This seems to us to fit more appropriately with our position on the uncertainty and mutability of traditional descriptions of categories of pupils with special educational needs. We have also gathered evidence of significant differences between the learning characteristics of pupils who have been offered similar diagnoses. As we shall see later, individual pupils described as being on the autistic continuum, for example, may be assessed as having more differences, in terms of their learning characteristics, than similarities.

In order to support this process of assessment, we developed and trialled a pupil profiling sheet (see Figure 4.2). It may be worth taking some time at this point to review some of the principles that lie behind this assessment tool.

Name:	Class:	Key Stage:

Biographical notes:

Learning profile:	*Ease*	*Comfort*	*Neutrality*	*Challenge*	*Frustration*	*Stress*

Other comments:

Figure 4.2 Pupil profiling sheet

The idea of a profile

We have borrowed the idea of a learner profile from a number of sources and built our own ideas upon it. In just the same way that Gardner (1993a; 1993b) rejects the view of intelligence in which pupils are either intelligent or not, authors in the field of learning style preference have developed ideas about learners taking up individual positions in relation to a range of possible styles (see Chapter 2 in this book; Riding and Rayner 1998; Read 1998). This suggests a more complex, and, we would argue, a more useful view of learning preferences than simply labelling one pupil as a 'wholist' and another as 'analyst' in style.

Kolb (1976), for example, describes learners as having characteristic patterns of preference across his four major typologies of learning style. Sternberg (1997), in his more complex analysis of individual style, function and form, argues that 'people have profiles (or patterns) of styles, not just a single style'. We wanted to find a way of profiling learners in order to make these individual patterns of learning preference explicit. We also wanted a system which was open-ended enough to allow for individual divergence and yet consistent enough to facilitate the sharing of information and potentially, as we shall see below, the involvement of learners themselves.

Working towards the comfort zone

The learning profile is designed to assess a pupil's preferences for learning in certain characteristic ways. It is not, however, simply another analysis of skills or competencies. As Sternberg (1997) says, 'styles are preferences in the use of abilities, not abilities themselves'. We have therefore provided, across the horizontal axis of our profile sheet, a graded continuum of affective response to learning. Other authors and practitioners also emphasise the significance of pupils' emotional responses to the demands of the learning situation (see, for example, Long 1999; Long and Fogell 1999). There are parallels here with what Hart (1996) in her analysis of 'innovative thinking' in relation to pupils with special educational needs, refers to as 'noting the impact of feelings' (see also LCAS 1999). We took the idea that learners may be 'comfortable' working in their own core or 'natural' style (Bennett 1976) but 'stressed' by being required to work in a style which conflicts with their preference from Butler (1995, 1997). We have, in the light of experience trialling this affective continuum with practitioners, extended it to encompass:

ease   comfort   neutrality   challenge   frustration   stress

At a simple level, we have suggested to practitioners that pupils may feel differently about working in different 'modalities' (Butler 1995, 1997). Thus a learner may feel at ease working from visually-orientated materials like pictures or symbols and significantly stressed by the prospect of following verbal instructions. The profile may therefore simply be used to build up a picture of a learner's preferences and areas of difficulty or conflict (see Figure 4.3). In our experience, this process can, in itself, be instructive. For instance, participants in our staff development sessions have been heard, on several occasions, experiencing moments of insight and noting, for example, that a pupil's behaviour always seems to get worse when there is written work to do.

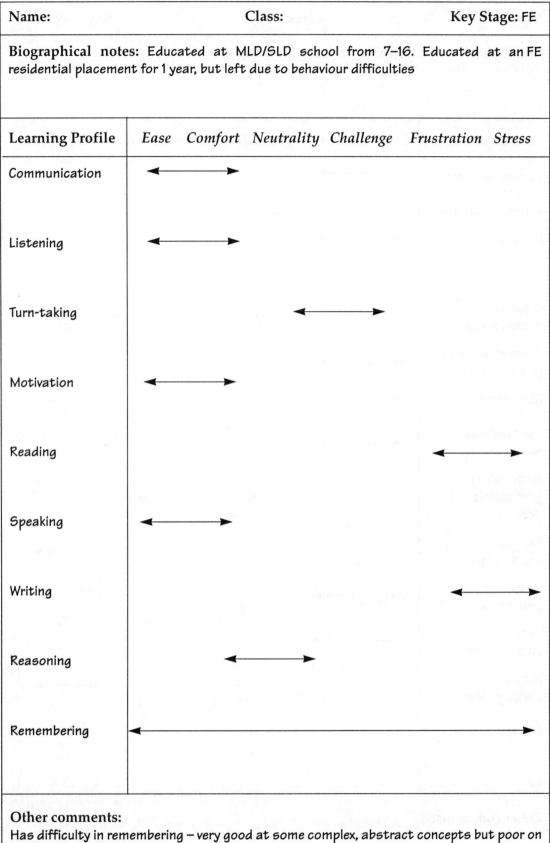

| Name: | Class: | Key Stage: FE |

Biographical notes: Educated at MLD/SLD school from 7–16. Educated at an FE residential placement for 1 year, but left due to behaviour difficulties

Learning Profile	*Ease*	*Comfort*	*Neutrality*	*Challenge*	*Frustration*	*Stress*
Communication	←——→					
Listening	←——→					
Turn-taking			←——→			
Motivation	←——→					
Reading					←——→	
Speaking	←——→					
Writing						←——→
Reasoning		←——→				
Remembering	←——————————————————————————→					

Other comments:
Has difficulty in remembering – very good at some complex, abstract concepts but poor on short term mundane information. Self-esteem has increased enormously since being given more responsiblity which has led to a decrease in behaviour difficulties.

Figure 4.3 Example of completed pupil profiling sheet

Name:	Class:			Key Stage: 2	
Biographical notes: English is his second language					
Learning Profile	*Ease* *Comfort*	*Neutrality*	*Challenge*	*Frustration*	*Stress*
Communication-3 word level; signing; illustrations	←——→				
Imitation	←——→				
Collaborative tasks (peers)					←——→
Joint attention (eye contact).	←——→				
Motivation.	←——→				
Routine/known structure.	←——→				
Active verbal participation of peers.		←——→			
Physical prompting.				←——→	
Verbal prompting.	←——→				
Active participation.	←——→				
Passive participation.				←——→	
Problem solving.	←——→				
Other comments:					

Figure 4.4 Another example of a completed pupil profiling sheet

These sorts of difficulties may occur when there is a mismatch between the learning processes which are entailed in the task provided and an individual learner's preferences and/or capabilities. Sternberg (1997) asserts, however, that 'a match between styles and abilities creates a synergy that is more than the sum of its parts'. In other words, learning is likely to happen most effectively and with fewest difficulties where there is a match between a pupil's learning preferences, their skills and capabilities, and the nature of the learning task provided. So a pupil who likes to work on tactile, practical activities, who has well-developed fine motor skills and who is given some detailed cutting and assembling tasks to do in a session devoted to design and technology is likely to enjoy his learning and to be successful. As Chamberlain *et al.* (1996) note, this could be described as 'teaching *with*' a pupil's learning preferences; a way of 'starting from where the child is' which takes account of learning style as well as pre-existing skills, knowledge and understanding; and a way of playing to pupils' strengths as learners. The learning profile analysis can be used in order to identify the degree of match between preferences, skills and tasks and therefore to increase the possibility of facilitating the creative synergy that Sternberg (1997) describes (see Figure 4.4).

It is clear that not all learning can follow this neat synergetic formula, however. We emphasise the importance of the affective quality of this ease–stress continuum because some pupils may feel quite at ease working in areas in which they are, frankly, unskilled. We have encountered examples of pupils who have reached a plateau, let us say, in their use of handwriting, and who are quite content to remain in occupation of this comfortable zone. It may be, for such a pupil, that some positive challenge needs to be injected into proceedings in order to promote progress and new learning and that becoming a sensitive source of challenge may be a role that an observant teacher can adopt. Again, the profile may help staff to identify these opportunities.

Exploring challenge and stress

As we have seen, difficulties may occur for learners where there is conflict between their learning preferences and the activities that teachers provide. Under these circumstances, learners may become frustrated or enter what Butler (1995, 1997) calls the 'stress zone'. In many instances, this will be because there is a mismatch between the demands of a task and the skills or competencies of a learner. We have already noted, for example, that a pupil experiencing difficulties with reading and writing may be stressed to the point of disruption by an imposed activity involving literacy skills. However, we have also encountered pupils who experience stress when working in areas in which they are, frankly, highly skilled. A pupil may be a fluent speaker yet prefer to remain silent rather than exposing himself to the stress of talking in the public arena of a classroom. Again, a learner may have highly developed capabilities in using information and communications technology yet remain quietly at the back of the learners grouped around the computer because he is frustrated by the social dominance of other, less capable but confident, pupils who have commandeered the keyboard and screen. It may be important for the teacher, under these circumstances, to understand the relationship between skills and other affective factors and to focus, for some individual learners, on issues like self-confidence, social fluency or self-esteem (see, for example, Gurney 1988; Lawrence 1988) in addition to seeking progress in the development of skills, concepts, knowledge and understanding.

In order to move beyond the simple analysis of learner preferences, then, we would argue that a learning profile should indicate some ways of working which a pupil is likely to find challenging. Chamberlain *et al.* (1996) describe this approach as 'teaching to enhance' while Honey and Mumford (1992) suggest that a controlled mismatch between style and task can actively stimulate growth and flexibility. The idea that learning preferences can, and do, change is an important one. Entwistle (1981) argues that pupils can be encouraged to modify their 'natural' style and that effective learners need to develop 'versatility' in their learning preferences. He further suggests that pupils might develop this versatility by engaging with contrasting learning opportunities deliberately provided by teachers. Sternberg (1997) argues that style preferences certainly change over time (so that the messy play explorer of the nursery may become a meticulous and methodical student in later years) and agrees that 'styles are teachable'. He suggests, for example, that young children observe style, and various strengths of style preference, in role models. As they grow older, they will thus become 'socialised' to certain style preferences and make these part of their repertoire as well as having innate preferences of their own.

Butler (1995, 1997) proposes that new preferences can develop as learners are encouraged to 'move easily' between their core attributes (comparable to Bennett's (1976) 'natural' style) and 'areas of versatility, flexibility and learned behaviours' in relation to their learning preferences. Butler describes the 'range of versatility' as a 'healthy and chosen place' which teachers can help to enlarge and illuminate for learners. She also proposes that teachers can help pupils to learn to cope with the stress of extreme mismatch or contrast for brief periods, developing strategies which will help them to extend their learning repertoires and drive back the boundaries that limit their learning. There are parallels here with Vygotsky's (1962) notion of the 'zone of proximal development', which Wood (1998) describes as the territory between what a learner is 'able to do alone' and what that same learner 'can achieve with help from one more knowledgeable or skilled than himself.' We discuss the important distinctions between direct help, support and guided participation below.

Sternberg (1997) also suggests that pupils will have learning preferences that 'are variable across tasks and situations'. In our work we have, for example, encountered pupils who are quite at ease with making a verbal response in a structured, one-to-one situation with an adult (suggesting, on a simple level, that they are comfortable verbalists) but who find communication within an interactive group extremely stressful. Such pupils may be helped to extend or generalise their preferred learning modes into new situations just as they can be encouraged to develop new ways of learning.

Thus challenge is not always to be avoided. Creating a flow of learning opportunities in which the learner is shielded from making mistakes and in which errors are absent, is to deny pupils the chance to learn from and to grow confident in the face of apparent failure. Experiencing the challenge of exploring and solving problems is an important aspect of learning if pupils are emotionally robust enough, or well enough supported by staff or peers (Charlton and Jones

1996), to cope with it. Teachers who know their pupils well will be able to judge the degree of challenge which may be appropriate in any given situation and, in Wood's (1998) phrase, 'determine whether or not instruction is *sensitive* to a child's zone of development'.

In summary

This section has made a number of points about learning preferences which we would summarise as follows:

- learning profiles are specific to individual pupils;
- learning profiles are not simply an analysis of skills – they have an affective dimension, showing a range of responses from ease to stress;
- learning will be most effective when there is a match between learning preferences and the task set;
- learning preferences can change and develop;
- pupils should be challenged to extend their learning into areas of challenge so that they are supported in becoming more versatile as learners;
- a good learning profile will encompass a balance of:
  - areas of learning in which the pupil feels at ease or comfortable;
  - areas of learning in which the pupil experiences some stress or is at least beginning to feel some challenge;
  - areas of learning in which the pupil is being supported in developing strategies for coping with extreme mismatch between preference and task.

Engaging with learning processes

If the horizontal axis of our learning profile invites staff to reflect on pupils' affective responses in a range of learning situations, the vertical axis is intended to promote thought and reflection about the range of learning processes which are significant at the time of the profile for an individual pupil. In order for profiles to be effective, we have suggested to colleagues that profiles should focus on a manageable number of learning processes at any one time. In this sense, we acknowledge a parallel with individual education planning in relation to the *Code of Practice* (DfE 1994). Ramjhun (1995), for example, suggests in this context that staff should avoid attempting 'to address all of the child's difficulties' at once. Ramjhun proposes, in contrast, a need to be 'selective and specific' in the development of individual education plans (IEPs) so that it is possible 'to focus on the priority problem and to ensure that the focus leads to identifiable results'.

We would encourage a similar approach to profiling. We have therefore deliberately offered profiles which are open-ended in terms of the learning processes with which they are concerned. We have encouraged staff to insert those headings, in the vertical axis of the profile, which they regard as relevant to individual pupils and their current strengths, needs and difficulties.

We regard the latter point as important. In our view, a good profile will capture the range of a pupil's performance across areas of full effectiveness and emerging confidence, as well as acceptable challenge and real difficulty. We have expressed this range of possibilities to participants in our project as encompassing:

- *experiences* – or areas of learning to which learners are exposed although they may be passive and/or their skills, knowledge, understanding or attitudes may be unknown or unestablished within such encounters;
- *learning activities* – or a variety of opportunities in which pupils become involved whether, at this stage, such involvement is supported, facilitated, guided, or encouraged by staff or peers and/or entails more active participation;
- *concepts and understandings* – whereby important constructs may begin to become confirmed for learners, as emerging schemes of action or pre-concepts, and/or as part of a working map of ideas;
- *skills and competencies* – which learners may acquire, maintain, consolidate, refine or generalise into new situations so that they develop the capability to reproduce, with varying degrees of consciousness and confidence, those behaviours which led to previous accomplishments;
- *strategies* – whereby learners select from a repertoire of learning options and, as a considered and deliberate policy, bring established knowledge, skills, understandings and attitudes to bear upon new challenges, problems and learning opportunities.

We provide a version of these notes, ready for copying or overhead projection, as Figure 4.5. Before we proceed with the discussion of the issues in practice, it may be worth consolidating our construction of this continuum by reference to the literature.

The relationships between experiences, ideas and concepts

Authors who work with pupils with profound and multiple learning difficulties have become increasingly interested in the significance of experience. The level descriptors provided by Brown (1996), for example, describe pupil outcomes in terms of the relationships between 'experiencing', 'awareness', 'responses', 'involvement' and 'participation'. This spectrum of possible outcomes compares interestingly with that given by McInnes and Treffry (1982). Although their work refers specifically to deaf-blind learners, they describe a series of stages of interaction between learners and their environment encompassing resistance, tolerance, passive cooperation, enjoyment, cooperative response, taking a lead, imitation and initiation which may have a wider application. For example, these ideas have since been used (Byers 1996; SCAA 1996; Ouvry and Saunders 1996) to give some form to the task of measuring the value of experiences to pupils with profound and multiple learning difficulties. This is work which confirms that progress towards the acquisition of skills, knowledge and understanding begins with experience.

Brown (1996) suggests that 'ideas will arise from pupils' own experience.' In this assertion, she builds on Piaget's seminal works on cognitive development and on the active and interactive nature of the relationship between the organism and the environment. Piaget argued that children, through their actions in relation to 'the immediate concrete situation', begin to construct 'pre-concepts' which have 'no abstract or formal elements' (Turner 1975). Piaget described the ways in which the learner assimilates information about the external world and accommodates this new information by making related changes to established

---

LEARNING to LEARN: from EXPERIENCE to STRATEGY

experiences – or areas of learning to which learners are exposed although they may be passive; and/or their skills, knowledge, understanding or attitudes may be unknown or unestablished within such encounters;

learning activities – or a variety of opportunities in which pupils become involved whether, at this stage, such involvement is supported, facilitated, guided, or encouraged by staff or peers; and/or entails more active participation;

concepts and understandings – whereby important constructs may begin to become confirmed for learners, as emerging schemes of action or pre-concepts, and/or as part of a working map of knowledge and ideas;

skills and competencies – which learners may acquire, maintain, consolidate, refine or generalise into new situations so that they develop the capability to reproduce, with varying degrees of consciousness and confidence, those behaviours which led to previous accomplishments;

strategies – whereby learners select from a repertoire of learning options and, as a considered and deliberate policy, bring established knowledge, skills, understandings and attitudes to bear upon new problems, challenges and learning opportunities.

Figure 4.5 Learning to learn

mental structures. He argued that 'schemes of action' in relation to environmental stimuli can be coordinated and developed into 'instinctual', 'sensory-motor', and 'operational' cognitive structures which he linked to his categorisation of cognitive development into the 'sensory-motor', 'pre-operational', 'concrete operational' and 'formal operational' stages of cognitive development (Piaget 1953).

Kolb (1984) proposed that the interactions between a learner and his experiences lie at the root of learning. He argued that 'learning is the process whereby knowledge is created through the transformation of experience' and that ideas and concepts are shaped and, over time and in the light of new encounters, reframed in response to experience. Schön (1991) describes a similar relationship, which we have used elsewhere in this text, between 'knowing-in-action' and 'reflecting-in-action'. We suggest here, then, that learners should not only be offered a range of experiences but also that they should be encouraged to move on from opportunities and encounters in which they are simply presented with the possibility of learning.

Learning activities

The development of the 'knowing-in-action', 'schemes of action' or 'pre-concepts' we have discussed above entails supporting pupils in becoming active participants in the processes that Riding and Rayner (1998) refer to as 'learning activities'. It is this supported involvement which helps to develop fully-fledged ideas and concepts and to build independent skills and competencies. Collis and Lacey (1996) draw a useful distinction between different forms of support. They discuss 'assistance', which entails giving the learner direct help to complete tasks; 'prompting', which is used to shape a learner's behaviour; and 'scaffolding', an idea developed by Wood *et al.* (1976), which involves supporting a learner in such a way that he is guided towards finding his own solutions to learning problems. Rogoff (1990) uses the term 'guided participation' to encompass those forms of learning support which:

- help learners to make connections between what they already know and can do and new challenges;
- contribute structure to learners' own problem solving;
- ensure active participation for the learner;
- focus on the transfer of control from teacher to learner.

It is this sort of guided participation which we wish to endorse.

Learning activities, in the sense in which we use this term, are not necessarily subject specific; indeed, the learning profile under discussion here does not set out to assess subject-related knowledge. However, some of the cross-curricular competencies which are included in the programmes of study for particular subjects (such as speaking and listening, reading or writing, using a computer keyboard, or sorting, grouping and classifying) may well be represented in a pupil profile. Similarly, the profile does not have to refer to the categories of cross-curricular or key skills, although many of these ideas (communicating, working with other people in groups or becoming a self-managing learner) may be very relevant to the development of an effective learning profile and may relate directly to targets within pupils' individual education plans (Caviglioli 1997; DfEE 1998a). We suggest that staff, in creating learning profiles, preferably in consultation and negotiation with colleagues and with individual learners, arrive at sets of categories which are truly relevant to the learning characteristics of individual pupils and students.

In support of this process, Mulligan (1992) offers an analysis of a range of internal processes which he considers to be crucial to learning through experience and which we discussed in more detail in Chapter 3. These entail:

willing   remembering   reasoning   feeling
sensing   intuiting   imagining

It is interesting to note that, although Mulligan's analysis of these processes emerged from the study of adult learners in higher education, they have proved to be entirely appropriate and applicable for pupils with learning difficulties. Wood (1998) states that attending, concentrating and remembering are also fundamental to learning. Gardner (1993a and 1993b) provides an analysis of multiple intelligences which he divides into seven categories:

linguistic   logical-mathematical   spatial   musical
bodily-kinaesthetic   interpersonal   intrapersonal

We have often usefully combined these intelligences (with the addition of a 'sensory' intelligence) with the learning processes provided by Mulligan and Wood in order to prompt staff during profiling. We make no claims for this as an exhaustive analysis of the learning activities which might be included in learner profiles – indeed, we acknowledge that we have deliberately emphasised ideas that may be of relevance to pupils with learning difficulties, but if readers suspect that they may find this breakdown useful, it is included here as Figure 4.6.

---

communicative
for example:
communicating by
using symbols, signing,
speaking, listening,
reading, writing

practical
for example:
reaching, holding,
grasping, moving,
controlling, making,
manipulating, doing

interpersonal
for example:
interacting, sharing,
turn-taking, perceiving
and interpreting others'
thoughts and feelings

spatial
for example:
perceiving, exploring,
creating, interrelating,
or sequencing 2D & 3D
pattern and form

analytical
for example:
sorting, grouping
comparing, classifying,
testing, quantifying,
counting, measuring

sensory
for example:
exploring by
looking, hearing, tasting,
touching, smelling

intrapersonal
for example:
willing, concentrating,
attending, remembering,
intuiting, imagining,
choosing, expressing
feelings & preferences

musical
for example:
perceiving, interpreting,
generating, responding
to pitch, harmony,
dynamics, rhythm,
tempo, texture, timbre

Figure 4.6 Learning processes (derived from Gardner's and Mulligan's analyses)

Skills and strategies

Having established a relationship, then, between experience, the processes fundamental to learning and the development of emerging concepts and understandings, we move on to consider the development of skills and competencies. This is an area of work in which teachers who work with pupils with learning difficulties tend to be more secure, as we have seen in Chapter 3. The behaviourist tradition, and the acknowledged value of skills based approaches like EDY (Farrell *et al.* 1992) and Portage (White and Cameron 1986), have secured the relationship between 'doing' and learning. White and Haring (1980) sum up this learning sequence (with acknowledgements to Cameron *et al.* 1986) as encompassing a number of phases which we detailed in Chapter 2.

It is interesting to note here that many pupils with learning difficulties may require extensive exposure to a range of experiences and to involvement in the sorts of learning activities which we have described above before they are able to acquire new skills in response to teaching methods like demonstration, modelling or even physical prompting. It is also worth remarking that this analysis indicates the value of 'doing' learning activities repeatedly, at first as routines under familiar circumstances but later challenging learners to extend their repertoire of skills into new, perhaps deliberately simulated, contexts.

The final phase of White and Haring's model brings us close to a useful working definition of learning strategies. Learners, they suggest, may become so confident and competent in the use of certain skills or in certain areas of understanding that they become able to apply these skills or understandings, or to adapt them in new and unfamiliar ways, to new and unfamiliar situations. Nisbet and Shucksmith (1986) define learning strategies as 'integrated sequences of procedures selected with a purpose in view'. They also suggest that successful learners will have 'developed a range of strategies from which they are able to select appropriately and adapt flexibly to meet the needs of a specific situation'. We have argued above that it is important for pupils to become comfortable with learning in an increasing variety of ways. Riding and Rayner (1998), building upon Pask's (1976) view of the importance of 'versatility' in learning, describe the development of 'a repertoire of learning strategies' moving:

- from an initial awareness of individual preferences for learning in certain ways;
- through an ability to select appropriate responses to given tasks;
- towards the capacity to adapt and extend learning in new situations and contexts.

Nisbet and Shucksmith (1986) note that strategies are generally regarded as being 'higher-order skills which control and regulate the more task-specific or more practical skills'. Riding and Rayner (1998), in their analysis of the work of a number of authors, argue that strategy use is defined by conscious decision-making, by motivation and intentionality. They offer a description of four levels of strategy formation:

- intuitive actions;
- low-level automated actions;
- deliberate and consciously extended actions;
- high-level automated actions.   (p. 88)

However, Nisbet and Shucksmith (1986) also note that it is possible, even common, for learners to employ strategies 'instinctively and probably unconsciously', without bringing an awareness of strategy use to 'a conscious or deliberate level', provided that they remain 'purposeful and goal-orientated'.

Balancing the profile

Is it possible, given these notions, that a pupil with profound and multiple learning difficulties can become a strategy user? We would suggest that the apparently hierarchical nature of the experience–strategy continuum does not preclude this possibility. We suggest that a range of responses to experiences and strategies, with all shades of options in between, should be recorded in profiles for all learners. Thus a learner with profound and multiple learning difficulties may use 'reaching out to touch' as a deliberate learning strategy, or at least as a 'deliberate and consciously extended action' (Riding and Rayner 1998), with which he is now entirely at ease. This pupil may have started out as a 'naturally' or 'instinctively' tactile defensive learner. We may imagine that he has been supported, by guided participation, through a range of experiences and co-active processes, many of which will have been very challenging for him, until he has arrived at a point where he can use his now-established confidence as a skilled 'reacher-toucher' with ease. This may have been possible only because his support staff understood his natural tendency to enjoy person-to-person interactions and were able to use this sense of ease to moderate the challenge of learning to reach and touch.

At the other end of the experience–strategy continuum, we might imagine a triple-A physics student who finds the prospect of the experience of a school trip to the opera extremely stressful. It may be possible for the physics student's music teacher, who wishes to encourage her pupil to engage with the challenge of an encounter with opera, to moderate the unfamiliarity of this experience by asking him to undertake a task which comes much more naturally to him in an area in which he is skilled and knowledgeable. She may, for example, ask him to research the complexities of the lighting board at the theatre as he listens to the music, because she knows he will feel at ease with this task, even as he is challenged by the new and unfamiliar experience of the performance.

We suggest, then, that staff can use the profiling process in order to ensure that all learners, including pupils with learning difficulties and those who are most gifted, are offered a range of learning opportunities which encompasses new experiences; supported involvement in unfamiliar activities; the further refinement of skills, knowledge and understanding; and the development of a growing repertoire of learning strategies. We would also suggest that the skilled profiler can jigsaw together (Rose 1991) the profiles of a number of learners in a group so that the involvement of one pupil in a new experience can be supported by the participation of other pupils who may have emerging understandings, established skills, or well-developed strategies for engaging with the task in hand. As Rogoff (1990) argues, these sorts of 'flexible webs of relationships that focus on shared cultural activities' can help to provide pupils with 'opportunities to participate in diverse roles' and, we suggest, to promote inclusion.

In summary

This section has made a number of points about learning processes which we would summarise as follows:

- learning profiles should focus on a manageable range of issues at any one time;
- learning profiles have a process dimension, showing a range of possibilities from experience to strategy use;
- experience could be said to underpin all learning;
- learners can be supported in becoming involved in a range of learning activities;
- learning profiles can be used to support the development of multiple intelligences;
- a good learning profile will encompass a balance of:
  - areas of learning in which the pupil engages with new experiences;
  - areas of learning in which the pupil is supported in engaging in a diversity of learning activities;
  - areas of learning in which the pupil is gaining or consolidating new skills and concepts;
  - areas of learning in which the pupil can develop new strategies for learning;
- where learners become aware of and involved in their own learning profiles, they can be encouraged to develop an extended repertoire of learning strategies.

How can pupils become self-aware and self-directing as learners?

One of the strategies we used in our work for this project entailed encouraging teachers to create profiles of themselves as learners. We believe, with Butler (1995, 1996, 1998), that the insights gained from this process will support staff in undertaking the profiling of pupils and in helping pupils to become more reflective about their own learning. As Butler says:

> In order to understand others, to teach with their needs in mind, and to design a meaningful and worthy curriculum, we look first to understand ourselves – our styles, needs, strengths, biases. We are most effective when we understand ourselves and our teaching, learn how we affect and influence others, and become aware how our actions may be part of a learner's problem, but more importantly, part of the solution. (p. 1)

We gave staff our standard learner profile (see Figure 4.2 p. 71), with appropriately adapted guidance, in one instance asking participants in a programme of further professional study at the University of Cambridge School of Education to profile themselves at the beginning and the end of a course focusing on techniques that might be used in school-based enquiry. The issues that these participants noted most frequently as causing them the most significant stress at the beginning of the course included working in groups, making presentations to colleagues and working with new people. The prospect of engaging in new experiences, like planning an enquiry, conducting interviews or analysing data, caused stress to many. Some participants also noted that they found writing, reading or using the computer challenging.

When given their original profiles back for comparison and reflection at the end of the course, participants recorded a general shift across the profile with regard to many of these processes from stress and challenge towards ease and comfort. Individual participants wrote comments on their second profiles, recording insights such as 'lost all my stresses!', 'do not feel so threatened now', or 'gradual immersing in new experiences . . . has been very helpful'. Some participants became more focused in their analysis of their own learning, noting that they had become comfortable, for example, working in small groups while still finding presentations to a large group of colleagues stressful. Interestingly, the course generated some new areas of stress and challenge, such as leading seminars, undertaking case studies, organising references or writing to deadlines. One participant noted, however, that there should be 'some positive concept of challenge/excitement of the new', indicating an acceptance of the notion that challenge can provide a useful and enjoyable impetus to new learning if appropriate support is available.

Learning to learn

These findings provide a useful illustration of many of the points we have made above about pupil profiling. We suggest that staff can take the insights gained from self-profiling into their work with pupils in schools and classrooms. Chamberlain *et al.* (1996), for example, discuss the possibility of making learners aware of their own profiles in order to expand their repertoire of learning strategies. Our findings also suggest that learner profiles might be used as an effective means of evaluating courses of study, especially where the development of skills for learning or study skills is an explicit purpose of the course. Nisbet and Shucksmith (1986) argue that staff should make the learning challenges within a task clear for pupils from an early age, by stating or describing them and, perhaps more effectively, through demonstration, modelling and prompting. They suggest that classroom practice often tends to focus on outcomes rather than on teaching learners how to learn by being explicit about learning strategies. Nisbet and Shucksmith (1986) argue that in order to use strategies effectively, learners need to 'be aware of what they are doing and of their own learning style, and to monitor their learning so as to be able to make appropriate decisions and to switch their choice if it appears to be ineffective'.

As we found with participants in the Cambridge course, learners who complete, or who are involved in completing, their own profiles are able to begin to monitor their own progress and development as learners. Nisbet and Shucksmith (1986) emphasise the importance of this process. They state that:

> many of the school programmes which teach more and more specifically differ-
> entiated skills and sub-skills are only ever likely to be partially successful. The
> acquisition and improvement of those skills may be an essential part of the school
> experience , but the factor which differentiates good from bad or inadequate learning
> is the ability to monitor situations, tasks and problems and respond accordingly, and
> this is an ability too rarely taught or encouraged in school. (p. 25)

Nisbet and Shucksmith's points may have a familiar ring for staff from special schools who, in the past, may have found themselves following skills-based checklists and achieving only partial success with their pupils. These teachers will understand the importance of locating skills-based learning in context. We now propose, with Nisbet and Shucksmith, that pupils should also be supported in gaining the knowledge, understandings, attitudes and capacity for self-awareness that will support the process of self-monitoring. We could identify this sort of self-awareness as being characteristic of the learner who knows how to learn.

Building upon the points we have made in the previous section about learners becoming strategy users, we note the work of Resnick and Beck (1976) who established the following principles and practices for teaching learning strategies to pupils:

- teach strategies in the context of subject-based knowledge, skills and understanding rather than in isolation;
- encourage a range of general strategies that can be applied across the curriculum;
- teach pupils how to organise, remember, recall and bring into use their prior learning;
- encourage pupils to:
  - become aware of their own learning processes;
  - use their most effective strategies consciously and deliberately in new situations;
  - monitor and organise their own learning.

Learning from the learner's perspective

Resnick and Beck's principles and practices remind staff to 'teach' or encourage a range of activities or processes. We would endorse many of these ideas, while acknowledging that they do not necessarily help practitioners to discover *how* to teach pupils to remember or to become aware of their own learning. Riding and Rayner (1998) provide a breakdown of the processes entailed in becoming a strategic learner from the pupil's point of view. They suggest that self-aware learning involves:

- creating a plan to reach a goal;
- selecting the specific strategies or methods to use to achieve a goal;
- implementing the methods selected to carry out the plan;
- monitoring progress on both a formative and a summative basis;
- modifying the plan, the methods, or even the original goal, if appropriate;
- evaluating the outcome in order to make a decision about further learning.

(p. 90)

As we discussed in Chapter 3, Nisbet and Shucksmith (1986) suggest that it is appropriate to envisage a 'continuum' of skills for learning across their hierarchy of micro, macro and central strategies and give an analysis of the pupil strategies which are 'most commonly mentioned' in the literature. Drawing upon the work of authors like Feuerstein (1979) and Sternberg (1983), their list encompasses:

- *asking questions* – defining hypotheses, establishing aims and parameters of a task, discovering audience, relating task to previous work, etc.;
- *planning* – deciding on tactics and timetables, reduction of task or problem into components: what physical or mental skills are necessary?

- *monitoring* – continuous attempt to match efforts, answers and discoveries to initial questions or purposes;
- *checking* – preliminary assessment of performance and results;
- *revising* – may be simple re-drafting or recalculation or may involve setting of revised goals;
- *self-testing* – final self-assessment both of results and performance on task.

(p. 28)

Nisbet and Shucksmith (1986) link this analysis of learning strategies to the notion of metacognition. The work of authors like Blagg *et al.* (1988) supports the possibility of developing thinking skills, or metacognition, in the mainstream of education while Lake (1989) and Quicke (1992) explore the potential that these ideas have for work among pupils with special educational needs. Most current examples of the development of metacognition in practice tend to rely heavily on language based approaches (see, for instance, Quicke and Winter 1994). The challenge of applying this way of conceptualising effective learning for pupils who experience learning difficulties remains.

Records of achievement and progress files

Work in the area of developing the records of achievement process and progress files has begun to indicate ways in which practitioners might engage with this challenge. This has involved using a variety of ways to encourage pupils to become more aware of their own learning styles, strengths and preferences. Lawson (1998), for example, devotes a whole section of her book to pupil involvement in record keeping. She establishes 'different levels of self-evaluation'. These move towards pupil involvement in target setting by working from simple factual recording of events; through the communication of preferences and choices; to the evaluation of strengths and weaknesses. She recommends encouraging pupils to consider 'what was difficult to do?' and 'what was I good at?' in order to promote learners' self-awareness. Lawson's examples of self-recording formats, using symbols or pictures as well as words, include:

- questions posed to pupils such as: 'my favourite activity was . . .' and 'why?';
- records of affective response, such as: 'activities I like', as well as evaluations of achievement and difficulty such as 'activities I do well' and 'activities I need help with';
- analysis of new learning and aspirations for future progress such as: 'this week I learned something new about . . .'; 'I would like to learn more about . . .'; and 'in the future I would like to . . .'

In summary

We suggest that staff will find it productive to adapt some of Lawson's methods in order to explore the extent to which pupils with learning difficulties can be encouraged to become more aware of their strengths as learners. The tutorial process, and the use of self-recording sheets, could focus on questions like, for example:

- *What do you like doing best?* Shared information about preferred activities and decisions made with regard to curricular options can be used to help pupils to become aware of their talents and intelligences.

- *Which members of staff do you like to work with?* Although staff may feel threatened by the idea of pupils identifying 'favourite' teachers, the clarification of preferred styles of support may provide significant insights into pupils' learning styles.

- *How do you like to communicate while you are working?* Pupils could be offered a range of options to prompt responses including: talking, listening, using symbols, signing, reading and writing, using a computer or other information and communications technologies, doing things together, just being with someone, or simply working quietly and independently.

- *How do you like to work?* Information about pupils' sociability as learners and their preferences for working on their own, paired with a member of staff or another pupil or in small or large groups can be used by staff to devise an optimum range of pupil groupings and by pupils to choose propitious working partnerships in various lessons.

- *Which pupils do you like to work with?* Again, insights into preferred working partnerships, group memberships, informal mentoring relationships or learning friendships may tell staff a great deal about the areas of learning in which a pupil likes to be supported.

- *What do you find helpful before you start work?* Individual pupils may prefer to hear about what to do; to be shown what to do; to discuss what needs to be done with others; to watch someone else working before they attempt the task; or to get instructions on paper. Responses to these prompts may give staff clues about pupils' approaches to the task of planning their work.

- *How do you like to plan your work?* Pupils could be prompted here to consider strategies like: asking questions about the task before they begin; thinking about the work they have to do; remembering work they have done in the past and considering their successes and difficulties; asking for support with aspects they recognise as challenging; sequencing the important aspects of a task; imagining a range of outcomes; or just getting on with things. Staff input could support pupils in developing more sophisticated approaches to planning.

- *What helps you to decide how to do your work?* Pupils could be encouraged to consider possibilities like: sharing ideas with other people; watching other people working for a while; exploring tools and resources; or remembering their approaches to similar tasks in the past.

- *What are you good at doing?* Pupils may be prompted here to think about their skills, preferences and strategies for learning, including a range of possibilities like: remembering ideas from previous lessons; making up new ideas; bringing two different ways of working together; putting ideas down on paper; working directly with tools, materials and real objects; or working with other people.

- *How good are you at keeping on working?* For some pupils, the interesting peripheral phenomena that occur during work sessions may become engrossing. Staff may be able to help pupils who tend to become side-tracked into tangential activities to find ways of prompting themselves to keep focusing back on the main task.

- *What helps you to keep working?* In response to this question, staff may discover that individual pupils may prefer to: talk about what they are doing while they work; get on with things quietly; do their work as quickly as possible; or become involved with what other people are doing.
- *How do you check that your work is going well?* Pupils might be prompted to consider: watching to see what other people are doing; asking staff if things are going well; remembering instructions; checking instructions that have been provided; remembering what they wanted to achieve at the start of the task; or comparing their own work with any finished product that has been discussed, displayed or demonstrated.
- *How do you feel when you get stuck?* It will be useful for staff to know whether individual pupils tend to worry, panic, keep on working although they know things are already going wrong, start getting really interested or give up in the face of developing difficulties and emerging problems.
- *What do you do when you get stuck?* Some pupils may have the confidence, under certain circumstances, to try to sort the problem out by themselves; others may feel more comfortable asking a member of staff for help; some pupils will enjoy working on the problem with their peers.
- *How good are you at changing your plans?* Pupils' willingness to adjust to new circumstances and changed eventualities within a task will be variable. It will be helpful for pupils to become aware of any tendency to perseverate and to be encouraged to learn new flexibilities.
- *How do you like to check your work when you have finished?* Some pupils may like to share their successes and difficulties with the class; others may prefer to check their own work against pre-determined criteria; some may like to have their work reviewed by a trusted peer; others may prefer to have their work checked by staff.
- *How do you like to check your own learning?* As well as reviewing outcomes to tasks, pupils should also be encouraged to consider preferred ways of evaluating their own effectiveness as learners by considering issues like: their willingness to stay on task; their capacity for remembering things or prompting their own memories; working with others; or working to time limits.

We are not proposing that all these questions should be asked of pupils at one sitting. We also recognise that responses to the questions in this script will vary, for many individual learners, from subject to subject and activity to activity. Acknowledging the complexity of responses to questions like these will, however, help to build effective learning profiles over time and over a variety of tasks. Pupil involvement may be secured through discussion, the use of signs and symbols or the review of photographs or video. Some pupils will be able to respond directly to the questions we provide. Under other circumstances, interpretations of individual approaches to learning provided by staff or peers acting as advocates may contribute to the development of a learner's self-awareness. Learners may then become involved in target setting which focuses on learning how to learn and encouraged to check their own responses, on future occasions, against those targets.

Changes in practice of the kind that we have discussed in this section will demand parallel changes in school culture. The focus of teaching will need to widen in order to encompass process as well as product. We would argue that this shift in focus will have to be accomplished as part of the process of moving towards a form of schooling which meaningfully includes pupils with learning difficulties. In the next section, we turn to the relationship between improved practice and cultural change and highlight the importance of dialogue and collaboration in facilitating these processes.

How can cultural change lead to improved practice?

Cultural change is generated and perpetuated through planned changes in organisational structures, processes and practices. It is the ability of a school to reflect, to learn and to problem-solve, which determines the quality of its response to diversity. In turn its response to diversity will determine the quality of teaching and learning for all. Implicit within the literature on school effectiveness is an agreed common list of factors, which constitute the necessary conditions for school development. Such factors include leadership of the head teacher, focus on teaching and learning, high expectations and clearly understood group mission.

Dyson (1994) outlines three dimensions to school effectiveness and suggests that all three must to be in evidence before school effectiveness is realised. These are:

- managerial – or direct action by the school management resulting in improved teacher response to diversity in pupil population;
- organisational – or a radical reconfiguration of the school as a learning and problem-solving organisation;
- sociopolitical – the most challenging and far-reaching, requiring fundamental redistribution of power within the school, the educational system and ultimately society, giving rise to a shift in values which promotes inclusion.

Dyson asks 'how does a school, which . . . is unable to learn, learn how to become a learning school?'

In order to tackle such a penetrating question it is helpful to make a clear distinction between school effectiveness and school improvement (Mortimore and Taggart 1993). The concept of 'improvement' is defined by Robinson (1993):

> I adopt a pragmatist view of improvement, whereby practice is said to be improved when problems that arise in the pursuit of our goals or the satisfaction of our needs are resolved in ways that enhance our ability to resolve other problems that we experience. (p. 7)

There exists a wealth of literature which describes the surface features of effective schools. Nevertheless, it remains unclear how other schools devise, select and adapt strategies which will work for them in bringing about improvement. It is not simply a question of emulating or attempting to replicate the outward manifestation of what appears to be the model 'effective' school. Causing change in schools is a formidable challenge to all involved. As Dyson (1994) notes, 'we need to be aware that the creation of a school that can learn to be effective for all may be a more complex and difficult process than at first appears.' Strategies for improvement will need tailoring to fit each school's individual situation and learning biography. Dyson's question refers to the school that is unaware of what it does not know and yet needs to know before thinking can move it forward. How can a school in this situation improve its practice?

Schools cannot simply 'go it alone'. Individual schools, like individual teachers, need to reflect. In order to reflect they need to engage in dialogue. Schools require reflective and focused engagement with other schools, external change agents such as consultants, advisers and colleagues in institutions of higher education. Such dialogue, particularly when associated with a specific experience or project, such as inspection or a radical centrally defined initiative, may serve as a catalyst for change, at least at the initial entry level of management. Thus, Dyson's managerial dimension is critical in instigating change leading to improved practice in classrooms. However, more than the OFSTED (1995) concept of 'a strong leader' is needed in order to network strategically with outside agents and identify and channel energy for change within the critical mass of the school. The skill of generating a questioning culture, which in turn leads to general dissatisfaction with current school conditions and cultivates collective courage to move into the unknown, is the key characteristic of transformational leadership.

The organisational dimension is best illustrated in the position held by Skrtic (1991). Essentially, the traditionally stratified departmental and curricular arrangement within a school, if unchallenged, is seen as serving to produce a highly restricted repertoire of response to pupil diversity. The school as an organisation reacts not to external challenge but instead in line with internal dynamics and self-interest. As such, 'specialist' departments and units emerge which assist in maintaining the status quo. The organisation reacting in such a way will tend towards classifying pupils in line with narrow credentialist value judgements, thereby generating pupil failure and self-fulfilling teacher attitudes. Alternatively, the school, through a radical process of reconfiguration, can view the exceptional pupil as a challenge and in response critically evaluate its own teaching practice with the intention of meeting diverse learning needs. Such reconfiguration allows a school to discover what it does not know but needs to know in order to include all pupils.

Schools will have difficulty in engaging in reflective dialogue unless they operate within a context of collaboration and support. The socio-political dimension should not be understated when considering ways of facilitating such inter-school cooperation. It is vital for schools to feel valued and to have their views heard at local, regional and national levels. In order to feel valued, schools need to know that they are able to influence policy change and assist in shaping the pattern of provision within the local, regional and indeed national education system. A number of diverse schools with a variety of backgrounds and practices coming together through the process of reflective dialogue focused upon teaching and learning is not so much a novel idea as a timely one. Such a coming together represents a spectrum of provision aimed at meeting a continuum of need and is potentially powerful in both educational and political terms. Schools must come to feel the benefit of networking and know that honest exchange and open sharing will move all forward as all have something to learn as well as something to offer. The process of inter-school dialogue should result in an overall system of inclusive provision shaped and informed not by simplistic dogma but instead by experience and reflective practice.

Successive governments have reduced the role of the local education authority

(LEA). It has come to be realised that improvement in teaching and learning requires the targeting of resources at and the delegating of increased responsibility to schools. School autonomy has come to be seen and indeed accepted as desirable. There has been and continues to be a shift in power. However, concerns have been raised in relation to the quality and consistency of provision for pupils with learning difficulties in the context of increased school autonomy. Such concern is lessened when considering the potential role of LEAs within the overall political arena of educational management.

Whether such things as target setting and monitoring should take place at central or local government level is no longer a useful debate. The point to be made clear is that target setting and monitoring need not take place at both levels. With the increased centralisation of standard setting and curriculum planning, there is no educational justification for LEAs to serve some sort of policing role for government. The role for the LEA, if there is to be a LEA, is to facilitate collaboration between and assist in the development of schools. The LEA should reflect schools' vision about the development of an inclusive educational system. It should work towards increasing the effectiveness of school networking and joint problem solving.

Successive governments have attached priority to the field of special needs as an area for radical change. Certainly from the 1993 Education Act, which heralded the *Code of Practice*, to the Labour government's *Programme of Action* (DfEE 1998a), no one associated with the field of learning difficulties could avoid the impact of such sustained and penetrating policy. Indeed it remains vital that those informed professionals who have worked hard to ensure quality provision for pupils with learning difficulties now take the opportunity to help shape the design and delivery of enhanced provision. Within the collaborative culture of inter-school developmental dialogue, the positive role of the special school or separate specialist provision is a necessary condition for effective change. Indeed, if such schools do not become proactive in this way they will not only fail to shape an effective, inclusive education system but they will potentially frustrate the realisation of such a vision. Special schools can become change agents.

As Rayner (1994) states in unequivocal terms:

> A special school which seeks to perpetuate, in dodo like fashion, a splendid isolation it may have enjoyed in the past, is doomed to extinction. A provision that shows its worth and places its centre of activity at the heart of a locally organised educational community is more likely to remain alive and well. The special school, and the support service, should aim to create a new interest in partnerships between schools, which may provide support for SEN in far more successful ways than was previously realised. Ideally this relationship is not one based on conflict and competition, but on mutual benefit, which involves a business-like organisation of provision, serving a clearly defined educational community. (p. 170)

The collaborative culture of schools that leads towards improved practice is characterised by: the internal structures in place and processes at work within individual schools, and the dialogical relationship between schools set within an agreed and understood value system.

The effects of inter-school collaboration

Individual schools that engage in collaborative dialogue with other schools not only improve on what they already do well but become able to see themselves as others see them. Through this process of self-reflection schools come to know what they need to know in order to radically evaluate and reconstruct their practice and question their fundamental purpose.

The concept of synergy applies as much to groups of schools as it does to groups of teachers. A collaborative group of schools is more than the sum of its constituent parts, or school members. The collaborative culture reinforces and enhances the individual school response to diversity while at the same time not diminishing the individual school responsibility to respond.

The collaborative strength of schools when channelled can be both educationally and politically powerful. Firstly, by responding to challenge collaboratively and within an agreed value system, such response transcends any self-interest which may be generated by market forces. Secondly, such groups of schools possess the ability to challenge established power arrangements within their own organisations and also the power distribution within the education system at local, regional or national level.

In summary

This section has attempted to describe the features necessary to shape an inclusive education system. These include the following:

- a school's ability to problem-solve will determine its response to diversity;
- strategies for improvement will be determined by school context and learning biography;
- schools need to engage in dialogue within the context of collaboration and support;
- schools must shape policy on inclusion within the context of the local, regional and national education system.

5 Conclusions and implications

What is entailed in managing change?

The previous section has addressed the linking theme of dialogue which we have developed as an integral aspect of change and development at a number of levels:

- dialogue between schools at local, regional and national levels;
- dialogue between teachers and other professionals, parents and carers;
- dialogue between staff and pupils and between pupils and their peers.

There must, at each level of activity, emerge an improved understanding of the theory and practice of change in schools. Esland (1972) identifies four factors which serve as necessary and sufficient conditions before change in schools can occur. Such factors underpin the understanding and meaning of change and apply equally to each level of activity.

Change involves social interaction

Relations between all parties to change must remain unambiguous in order to promote direct dialogue and reduce confusion, tension and frustration. The relationship, for example, that LEAs have with government and schools is often unclear, giving rise to uncertainty and potential role conflict. When, for example, is the LEA a purchaser or provider of SEN services? Genuine discussion involving both speaking and listening must occur between ministers, managers and practitioners. A change of proposed policy through the process of consultation does not constitute a U-turn and should not be perceived as backing-down but as a consultative and considered response to constructive comment.

Change is a process

All need to appreciate that effective change is an ongoing process and requires measured and sustained effort over time. The proliferation of new policies from government suggests that ministers possess a less than developed understanding of the theory of change. Government cannot go it alone. Government needs to recognise that legislation alone will not cause effective change. Government needs to recognise that a 'one size fits all' approach to schools will not generate desired results.

Change disturbs the status quo

Inclusion inevitably will lead to a reshaping of schooling. As such the organisation and the nature of all schools must change. Individual schools cannot go it alone. Schools must transcend self-interest and together respond positively to local diversity. Participants will feel less threatened if they understand the change and regard it as real reform. Within schools, head teachers must involve all staff in the school development planning process. Such involvement will ensure that the school development plan is truly embedded within the culture of the school. Policies that rest on shared values will transform school organisation, structures and practice.

Change is the subject of individual perceptions

Social reality is shaped by personal experience and position within the educational system. Individual perceptions will be influenced by others' views shared through discussion, collaboration and joint problem solving. Teachers cannot go it alone. Individual perception will vary less if the consultative process within policy production, implementation and review is well balanced and opportunity for reflection and dialogue is encouraged by management and government.

What is the significance of critical dialogue?

We suggest that participating in these forms of dialogue also entails engaging in a process of self-reflection or internal dialogue for all those involved. According to Ainscow (1991) among others, 'improving schools and schools working towards inclusion will encourage teachers to adopt a reflective attitude towards their own practice'. Ainscow wants: 'teachers to analyse and reflect upon their own classrooms. Their concern should be with particular children as they interact with particular tasks and processes.' This process of self-reflection in turn entails, for all participants, self-awareness and self-questioning. We would suggest that the kind of critical dialogue (Robinson 1993) which we have espoused in our work is characterised by:

- a willingness to ask challenging questions without looking for simplistic answers;
- acceptance and celebration of uncertainty;
- an ongoing process of clarifying meanings and understandings.

In approaching our work for this project, we have furnished ourselves with a problem and attempted to explore the issues. We recognise that there are no easy solutions but we have, as Robinson (1993) proposes, engaged in the process of reformulating the problem. We have conducted an experiment, as much with our own understandings of the nature of the problem as with outcomes. This has led us to further questions and different problems, of course. At least we now have more insight into the issues and this, we would suggest, can be of practical use in our own work and beyond. We accept that the tests of the utility of our tentative results, in Schön's (1991) terms, lie in the future, as schools of all varieties attempt to meet the challenge of inclusion. We hope to be able to continue to develop our own practice and to contribute, in a spirit of enquiry, to the ongoing debate about including pupils with learning difficulties.

Although we regard the open-ended nature of our enquiry as healthy and productive, we hope that we have established the idea that inclusion is not solely about pupil placement. The construction of some ideologically driven and fixed end state in which all pupils are educated in a uniform way in uniform classrooms will not serve the best interests of learners. We would argue that the task of working towards inclusion means developing a new mindset that will allow constant re-invention of practice to meet the needs of successive generations of new and different individual pupils. Indeed, it is the quality of the dialogue that takes place between policy makers, parents, practitioners and learners that will define progress in this task. We contend that special schools and specialist staff have a vital role to play in this dialogue.

What does the specialist sector have to offer?

In our discussion of approaches to teaching and learning for pupils with learning difficulties, we have identified a number of strengths of practice in the specialist sector which, we argue, will make a significant contribution to the development of 'an increasingly inclusive education system' (DfEE 1998a). We can summarise these issues in the three broad categories of *collaboration*, *case work* and *curriculum*.

Collaboration

We would argue that colleagues in special schools have developed expertise in working in professional partnerships. The work of Lacey and Lomas (1993), Lacey (1998), Fox (1998) and Balshaw (1999) details and celebrates those practices which enable teachers, support staff and other professionals to work together in effective cooperation to the benefit of pupils with learning difficulties. As the process of promoting inclusion moves forward, these practices and their related skills, understandings and attitudes can be called upon to:

- promote positive interactions between school staff and other professionals which are focused on pedagogy, in the ways which we have described in this book, as well as paramedical issues;
- help specialist staff to support the work of their colleagues in mainstream classrooms;
- contribute to the development of new professional roles for specialist teachers as sources of advice, guidance and expertise and for support staff as increasingly well-qualified educators in their own right.

Staff in special schools have also developed expertise in working with families. Hornby (1994), Gascoigne (1995) and Lambe (1998) discuss the details of practices which could be said to promote effective home–school liaison in partnerships which have been stimulated by the requirements of the annual review cycle (DfE 1994). Arguably, these practices will become even more important as pupils with learning difficulties enter the mainstream environment where professional contact with parents, carers and siblings has been more limited and where the increasing significance of outcomes for whole cohorts of pupils may have clouded the view of the individual pupil and his family.

We have also noted above the progress which colleagues in special schools have begun to make in working in negotiation and partnership with pupils. Much of this work has involved developments in the uses of symbols (Detheridge and Detheridge 1997); alternative and augmentative forms of communication (Latham and Miles 1997; Coupe O'Kane and Goldbart 1998); and pupil involvement in assessment recording and target setting (Lawson 1998). This is a debate which is in progress and it concerns practices which are frequently innovative, often experimental, and certainly still evolving. As participants in the project which this book summarises, we identify this as an area for further study and practical exploration. Collaboration and partnership between practitioners and pupils, and between pupils and their peers, will, we are convinced, continue to be a key theme in an increasingly inclusive future.

Case work

The theme of partnership finds expression, for staff in specialist contexts, in the case work aspect of their practice. Authors like Sanderson (1998), Tilstone and Barry (1998) and Rose (1998) argue for the empowering nature of negotiated planning and learning and make connections with the established role of advocacy in the education of pupils with learning difficulties (Mittler 1996). Caviglioli (1997) and Reynolds and Caviglioli (1999) demonstrate how priorities for individual learners, established in plans for the education of individual pupils, can be expressed as cross-curricular targets in key areas of learning for pupils with learning difficulties. In this book we have explored the ways in which the case work dimension of education for pupils with learning difficulties may begin to take account of skills for learning as well as skills for life and of individual learning strengths, preferences and styles through the profiling process we have described. The insights that can be gained from these ways of working, and the skills of specialist staff in assessment and target setting, for example, should again be called upon, we propose, in support of the development of inclusive practice.

Curriculum

Returning finally to the subject of teaching and learning, we have noted above the extensive body of work which has emerged from the specialist sector with regard to promoting not only access to various subjects, but also meaningful participation and achievement within the curriculum. While the process of curriculum development and redefinition in special schools has generated many useful books and articles, we are aware, as practitioners and visitors to many special schools around the country, that this literature has mainly served to liberate subject coordinators and classroom staff to undertake their own imaginative and effective approaches to the implementation of the curriculum for pupils with learning difficulties. Practice is now hugely diverse. Small steps analyses, the work of the EQUALs movement, multi-modal approaches and the development of meticulously differentiated schemes of work all enable pupils with a wide range of skills, interests, difficulties and prior achievements to engage with new learning experiences and to demonstrate progress within an inclusive curriculum framework.

Further, the view of the curriculum which obtains in the specialist sector tends to encompass a well-rounded perspective on the whole curriculum. Specialist staff do not regard breadth and balance as only involving subjects. They are also concerned, appropriately, with pupils' physical, emotional, spiritual or personal and social development as central influences on the curriculum. They provide a wide range of learning opportunities, developed in order to secure relevance to pupils' adult lives, and recognise, record and celebrate, with their pupils, a wide range of outcomes. Hopefully the extent to which these outcomes include nationally validated forms of accreditation will be extended as increased inclusivity promotes access for pupils with learning difficulties to mainstream subject expertise and resources. At the same time, other forms of outcome, reflecting targets in pupils' individual education plans, for example, will continue to be important as will the expertise of specialist staff in implementing the whole curriculum to the advantage of individual pupils.

The focus of this book has been upon teaching and learning, however, and we have sought to demonstrate that this is another area of expertise which has been developed and which is developing within specialist contexts. Again, we suggest, the processes of thinking about teaching in an informed, reflective and critical way and entering into professional discourse with colleagues about these issues will be crucial to the success of inclusive practice. We have also noted the challenging possibility of learners developing their capacity to:

- participate in learning activities;
- develop skills for learning;
- become aware of themselves as learners

in order to develop emerging and established strategies for effective learning. As one of the St John's School phase facilitators said, 'I feel quite strongly that the pupils should have more of a voice in what they are doing, why they are doing it and how they are doing it'. We would argue that these ways of thinking and doing should continue to be developed through dialogue and collaboration between staff in the specialist sector and colleagues in the mainstream of education.

References

Ainscow, M. (1991) 'Effective schools for all: an alternative approach to special needs in education', in Ainscow, M. (ed.) *Effective Schools for All*. London: David Fulton Publishers.

Ainscow, M. and Hart, S. (1992) 'Moving practice forward', in *Support for Learning* 7(3), 115–120.

Ashdown, R., Carpenter, B. and Bovair, K. (1991) *The Curriculum Challenge: access to the National Curriculum for pupils with learning difficulties*. London: The Falmer Press.

Balshaw, M. (1999) *Help in the Classroom* (2nd edn). London: David Fulton Publishers.

Baron, J. (1978) 'Intelligence and general strategies', in Underwood, G. (ed.) *Strategies in Information-Processing*. London: Academic Press.

Bennett, N. (1976) *Teaching Styles and Pupil Progress*. London: Open Books.

Billinge, R. (1988) 'The objectives model of curriculum development: a creaking bandwagon?' *Mental Handicap* 16, 26–29.

Blagg, N., Ballinger, M. and Gardner, R. (1988) *Somerset Thinking Skills Course*. Oxford: Blackwell.

Brake, T., Perra, E. and Glenn, J. (1986) *Tools for Learning – information skills and learning to learn in secondary schools*. London: The British Library Board.

Brown, E. (1996) *Religious Education for All*. London: David Fulton Publishers.

Butler, K. A. (1995, 1997) *The Strategy Chart for Learning Styles, Levels of Thinking and Performance*. Columbia, CT: The Learner's Dimension.

Butler, K. A. (1995, 1996, 1998) *Viewpoints*. Columbia, CT: The Learner's Dimension.

Byers, R. (1990) 'Topics: from myths to objectives.' *British Journal of Special Education* 17(3), 109–112.

Byers, R. (1994a) 'Teaching as dialogue: teaching approaches and learning styles in schools for pupils with learning difficulties.' In Coupe O'Kane, J. and Smith, B. (eds) *Taking Control – enabling people with learning difficulties*. London: David Fulton Publishers.

Byers, R. (1994b) 'Providing opportunities for effective learning', in Rose, R. *et al.* (eds) *Implementing the Whole Curriculum for Pupils with Learning Difficulties*. London: David Fulton Publishers.

Byers, R. (1994c) 'The Dearing Review of the National Curriculum.' *British Journal of Special Education* 21(3), 92–96.

Byers, R. (1996) 'Classroom processes', in Carpenter, B., Ashdown, R. and Bovair, K. (eds) *Enabling Access – effective teaching and learning for pupils with learning difficulties*. London: David Fulton Publishers.

Byers, R. (1999) 'The National Literacy Strategy and pupils with special educational needs.' *British Journal of Special Education* 26(1), 8–11.

Byers, R. and Rose, R. (1996) *Planning the Curriculum for Pupils with Special Educational Needs: a practical guide*. London: David Fulton Publishers.

Cameron, R. J., Owen, A. J. and Tee, G. (1986) 'Curriculum management (part 3): assessment and evaluation.' *Educational Psychology in Practice*. October, 3–9.

Carpenter, B. and Ashdown, R. (1996) 'Enabling access', in Carpenter, B., Ashdown, R. and Bovair, K. (eds) *Enabling Access: effective teaching and learning for pupils with learning difficulties*. London: David Fulton Publishers.

Carpenter, B., Ashdown, R. and Bovair, K. (eds) (1996) *Enabling Access: effective teaching and learning for pupils with learning difficulties*. London: David Fulton Publishers.

Carr, W. and Kemmis, S. (1986) *Becoming Critical: education, knowledge and action research*. London: Falmer.

Caviglioli, O. (1997) 'Making it work.' *Special Children*. October, 15–19.

Chamberlain, V., Hopper, B. and Jack, B. (1996) *Starting Out MI Way: a guide to multiple intelligences in the primary school*. Bolton: D2.

Charlton, T. and Jones, K. (1996) 'Peer support practices in classrooms and schools', in Jones, K. and Charlton, T. (eds) *Overcoming Learning and Behaviour Difficulties: partnership with pupils*. London: Routledge.

Clark, C., Dyson, A., Millward, A. J. and Skidmore, D. (1997) *New Directions in Special Needs: innovations in mainstream schools*. London: Cassell.

Collis, M. and Lacey, P. (1996) *Interactive Approaches to Teaching: a framework for INSET*. London: David Fulton Publishers.

Cooper, P. (1999) 'The further evolution of emotional and behavioural difficulties: bringing the biopsychosocial approach into education', in Cooper, P. (ed.) *Understanding and Supporting Children with Emotional and Behavioural Difficulties*. London: Jessica Kingsley Publishers.

Coupe O'Kane, J. and Goldbart, J. (1998) *Communication Before Speech: development and assessment*, (2nd edn). London: David Fulton Publishers.

Coupe O'Kane, J. and Smith, B. (eds) (1994) *Taking Control: enabling people with learning difficulties*. London: David Fulton Publishers.

Creese, A., Norwich, B. and Daniels, H. (1998) 'The prevalence and usefulness of collaborative teacher groups for SEN: Results of a national survey' *Support for Learning* **13**(3), 109–114.

DES (Department of Education and Science) (1978) *Special Educational Needs: report of the committee of inquiry into the education of handicapped children and young people* (The Warnock Report). London: HMSO.

DES (Department of Education and Science) (1981) *Education Act*. London: HMSO.

DfE (Department for Education) (1994) *Code of Practice on the Identification and Assessment of Special Educational Needs*. London: DfE.

DfEE (Department for Education and Employment) (1998a) *Meeting Special Educational Needs: a Programme of Action*. London: DfEE.

DfEE (Department for Education and Employment) (1998b) *The National Literacy Strategy Framework for Teaching*. London: DfEE.

DfEE (Department for Education and Employment) (1998c) *The National Literacy Strategy Framework for Teaching (Additional Guidance): Children with Special Educational Needs*. London: DfEE.

DfEE (Department for Education and Employment) (1999) *The National Numeracy Strategy Framework for Teaching Mathematics from Reception to Year 6*. London: DfEE.

Dearing, Sir R. (1993) *The National Curriculum and its Assessment: Final Report*. London: SCAA.

Detheridge, T. and Detheridge, M. (1997) *Literacy Through Symbols: improving access for children and adults*. London: David Fulton Publishers.

Dyson, A. (1994) 'Towards a collaborative, learning model for responding to student diversity', *Support for Learning* **9**(2), 53–59.

Entwistle, N. (1981) *Styles of Teaching and Learning: an integrated outline of educational psychology for students, teachers and lecturers*. London: David Fulton Publishers.

Esland, G. M. (1972) 'Innovation in the school', in Seaman, P., Esland, G.M. and Cosin, B. (eds) *Innovation and Ideology*. Milton Keynes: Open University Press.

FEFC (Further Education Funding Council) (1996) *Inclusive Learning: principles and recommendations: a summary of the findings of the learning difficulties and/or disabilities committee* (The Tomlinson Report). Coventry: FEFC.

Fagg, S. and Skelton, S. (1990) *Science for All*. London: David Fulton Publishers.

Farrell, P. (1992) 'Behavioural teaching: a fact of life?' *British Journal of Special Education*. **19**(4), 145–148.

Farrell, P., McBrien, J. and Foxen, T. (1992) *EDY Instructor's Handbook*, (2nd edn.). Manchester: Manchester University Press.

Feiler, A. and Thomas, G. (1988) 'Special needs: past, present and future', in Thomas, G. and Feiler, A. (eds) *Planning for Special Needs: a whole school approach*. Oxford: Basil Blackwell.

Feuerstein, R. (1979) *The Dynamic Assessment of Retarded Performers*. Baltimore, Maryland: University Park Press.

Fox, G. (1998) *A Handbook for Learning Support Assistants: teachers and assistants working together*. London: David Fulton Publishers.

Foxen, T. and McBrien, J. (1981) *EDY Trainee Workbook*. Manchester: Manchester University Press.

Friere, P. (1972) *Pedagogy of the Oppressed*. Harmondsworth: Penguin.

Fullan, M. (1991) *The New Meaning of Educational Change*, (2nd edn). London: Cassell.

Gardner, H. (1993a) *Frames of Mind*, (2nd edn). London: Fontana.

Gardner, H. (1993b) *The Unschooled Mind: how children think and how schools should teach*. London: Fontana.

Garner, P., Hinchcliffe, V., and Sandow, S. (1995) *What Teachers Do: developments in special education*. London: Paul Chapman Publishing.

Gascoigne, E. (1995) *Working with Parents as Partners in SEN*. London: David Fulton Publishers.

Glaser, B. G. and Strauss, A. L. (1967) *The Discovery of Grounded Theory*. Chicago: Aldine.

Griggs, S. A. (1991) *Learning Styles Counselling*. Ann Arbor, MI: ERIC Counselling and Personnel Services clearing house, University of Michigan.

Gurney, P. W. (1988) *Self-Esteem in Children with Special Educational Needs*. London: Routledge.

Hamblin, D. H. (1981) *Teaching Study Skills*. Oxford: Basil Blackwell.

Handy, C. (1985) *Understanding Organisations*. Harmondsworth: Penguin.

Handy, C. and Aitken, R. (1986) *Understanding Schools as Organisations*. Harmondsworth: Penguin

Hardwick, J. and Rushton, P. (1994) 'Pupil participation in their own records of achievement', in Rose, R. *et al.* (eds) *Implementing the Whole Curriculum for Pupils with Learning Difficulties*. London: David Fulton Publishers.

Hargreaves, D. (1999) 'Ask the experts', in *Times Educational Supplement,* February 12 p. 17.

Harris, A. (1996) 'Effective Teaching', in *School Improvement Network Bulletin*. London: Institute of Education.

Hart, S. (1996) *Beyond Special Needs: enhancing children's learning through innovative thinking*. London: Paul Chapman Publishing.

High/Scope Press (1991) *High/Scope K–3 Curriculum Guide Series*. Michigan, USA: The High/Scope Press.

Honey, P. and Mumford, A. (1992) *The Manual of Learning Styles (revised version)*. Maidenhead: Peter Honey.

Hopkins, D. (1997) 'Introduction', in Hopkins, D., West, M., Ainscow, M., Harris, A. and Beresford, J. *Creating the Conditions for Classroom Improvement*. London: David Fulton Publishers.

Hopkins, D., West, M. and Ainscow, M. (1996) *Improving the Quality of Education For All: progress and challenge*. London: David Fulton Publishers.

Hopkins, D., West, M., Ainscow, M., Harris, A. and Beresford, J. (1997) *Creating the Conditions for Classroom Improvement*. London: David Fulton Publishers.

Hornby, G. (1994) *Counselling in Child Disability: skills for working with parents*. London: Chapman and Hall.

Joyce, B. (1992) 'Co-operative learning and staff development: teaching the method with the method', *Co-operative Learning* **12**(2), 10–13.

Joyce, B. and Showers, B. (1988) *Student Achievement Through Staff Development*. New York: Longman.

Kessissoglou, S. and Farrell, P. (1995) 'Whatever happened to precision teaching?' *British Journal of Special Education* **22**(2), 60–63.

Kirby, J. R. (ed.) (1984) *Cognitive Styles and Educational Performance*. New York: Academic Press.

Kolb, D. A. (1976) *Learning Style Inventory: technical manual*. Englewood Cliffs, NJ: Prentice Hall.

Kolb, D. A. (1984) *Experiential Learning: experience as a source of learning and development*. Englewood Cliffs, NJ: Prentice Hall.

LCAS (Language and Curriculum Access Service) (1999) *Enabling Progress in Multilingual Classrooms*. Enfield, London: LCAS.

Lacey, P. (1998) 'Meeting complex needs through collaborative multidisciplinary teamwork', in Lacey, P. and Ouvry, C. (eds) *People with Profound and Multiple Learning Disabilities: a collaborative approach to meeting complex needs*. London: David Fulton Publishers.

Lacey, P. and Lomas, J. (1993) *Support Services and the Curriculum: a practical guide to collaboration*. London: David Fulton Publishers.

Lake, M. (1989) 'Mind games in Milton Keynes.' *Special Children*. February, 20–23.

Lambe, L. (1998) 'Supporting families', in Lacey, P. and Ouvry, C. (eds) *People with Profound and Multiple Learning Disabilities: a collaborative approach to meeting complex needs*. London: David Fulton Publishers.

Landrus, R. I. and Mesibov, G. B. (undated) *Structured Teaching*. University of North Carolina: Division TEACCH.

Latham, C. and Miles, A. (1997) *Assessing Communication*. London: David Fulton Publishers.

Lawrence, D. (1988) *Enhancing Self-Esteem in the Classroom*. London: Paul Chapman Publishing.

Lawson, H. (1992) *Practical Record Keeping for Special Schools*. London: David Fulton Publishers.

Lawson, H. (1998) *Practical Record Keeping: development and resource material for staff working with pupils with special educational needs*, (2nd edn.). London: David Fulton Publishers.

Lewis, A. (1992) 'From planning to practice', *British Journal of Special Education* 19(1), 24–27.

Lewis, A., Neill, S. and Campbell, J. (1996) '"It doesn't concern us!" The *Code of Practice* and its relevance for special schools, units and services', *British Journal of Special Education* 23(3), 105–109.

Lewis, J. E. and Wilson, C. D. (1996) *Pathways to Learning in Rett Syndrome*. London: UK Rett Syndrome Association.

Lincoln, Y. S. and Guba, E. G. (1985) *Naturalistic Inquiry*. Newbury Park and London: Sage.

Long, R. (1999) 'The heart of the matter', *Special!* Spring 1999, 12–15.

Long, R. and Fogell, J. (1999) *Supporting Pupils with Emotional Difficulties: creating a caring environment for all*. London: David Fulton Publishers.

MEC Teacher Fellows (1990) *Entitlement for All in Practice: a broad, balanced and relevant curriculum for pupils with severe and complex learning difficulties in the 1990s*. London: David Fulton Publishers.

McInnes, J. M. and Treffry, J. A. (1982) *Deaf-Blind Infants and Children: a developmental guide*. Toronto: University of Toronto Press.

McNamara, S. and Moreton, G. (1997) *Understanding Differentiation: a teachers' guide*. London: David Fulton Publishers.

Miller, A. and Watts, P. (1990) *Planning and Managing Effective Professional Development: a resource book for staff working with children who have special needs*. Harlow: Longman.

Mittler, P. (1996) 'Preparing for self-advocacy', in Carpenter, B., Ashdown, R. and Bovair, K. (eds) *Enabling Access: effective teaching and learning for pupils with learning difficulties*. London: David Fulton Publishers.

Morgan, J., Ashbaker, B., Forbush, D. (1998) 'Strengthening the teaching team: teachers and paraprofessionals learning together', *Support for Learning* 13(3), 115–117.

Mortimore, P. and Taggart, B. (1993) 'Where next?', *Managing Schools Today* 3(1) 12–14.

Mount, H. and Ackerman, D. (1991) *Technology for All: the development of cross-curricular skills with a thematic approach*. London: David Fulton Publishers.

Mulligan, J. (1992) 'Internal processors in experiential learning', in Mulligan, J. and Griffin, C. (eds) *Empowerment through Experiential Learning: explorations of good practice*. London: Kogan Page.

NCC (National Curriculum Council) (1989) *Curriculum Guidance 2: A Curriculum for All: special educational needs in the National Curriculum*. York: NCC.

NCC (National Curriculum Council) (1990) *Curriculum Guidance 3: The Whole Curriculum*. York: NCC.

NCC (National Curriculum Council) (1992) *Curriculum Guidance 9: The National Curriculum and Pupils with Severe Learning Difficulties*. York: NCC.

Nind, M. and Hewett, D. (1994) *Access to Communication: developing the basics of communication with people with severe learning difficulties through Intensive Interaction*. London: David Fulton Publishers.

Nisbet, J. and Shucksmith, J. (1986) *Learning Strategies*. London: Routledge and Kegan Paul.

O'Brien, T. (1998) *Promoting Positive Behaviour*. London: David Fulton Publishers.

OFSTED (Office for Standards in Education) (1995) *The Ofsted Handbook: Guidance on the Inspection of Special Schools*. London: HMSO.

Ouvry, C. (1987) *Educating Children with Profound Handicaps*. Kidderminster: BIMH.

Ouvry, C. and Saunders, S. (1996) 'Pupils with profound and multiple learning difficulties', in Carpenter, B., Ashdown, R. and Bovair, K. (eds) *Enabling Access: effective teaching and learning for pupils with learning difficulties*. London: David Fulton Publishers.

Pask, G. (1976) 'Styles and strategies of learning', *British Journal of Educational Psychology* 46, 128–148.

Piaget, J. (1953) *The Origin of Intelligence in the Child*. London: Routledge and Kegan Paul.

Powney, J. and Watts, M. (1987) *Interviewing in Educational Research*. London: Routledge and Kegan Paul.

Quicke, J. (1992) 'Clear thinking about thinking skills'. *Support for Learning*, 7(4), 171–176.

Quicke, J. and Winter, C. (1994) 'Teaching the language of learning: towards a metacognitive approach to pupil empowerment', *British Educational Research Journal* 20(4), 429–445.

Ramjhun, A. F. (1995) *Implementing the Code of Practice for Children with Special Educational Needs: a practical guide*. London: David Fulton Publishers.

Rayner, S. (1994) 'Restructuring reform: choice and change in special education', in *British Journal of Special Education* 21(4) 169–172.

Read, G. (1998) 'Promoting inclusion through learning styles', in Tilstone, C., Florian, L. and Rose, R. (eds) *Promoting Inclusive Practice*. London: Routledge.

Resnick, L. and Beck, I. L. (1976) 'Designing instruction in reading: interaction of theory and practice', in Guthrie, J. T. (ed.) *Aspects of Reading Acquisition*. Baltimore, Md: Johns Hopkins University Press.

Reynolds, B. and Caviglioli, O. (1999) 'Aiming true', *Special Children*. January, 25–28.

Riding, R. and Rayner, S. (1998) *Cognitive Styles and Learning Strategies: understanding style differences in learning and behaviour*. London: David Fulton Publishers.

Robinson, V. (1993) *Problem-Based Methodology: research for the improvement of practice*. Oxford: Pergamon Press.

Robson, R. (1993) *Real World Research: a resource for social scientists and practitioner-researchers*. Oxford: Blackwell.

Rogers, C. (1983) *Freedom to Learn for the 80s*. Columbia, Ohio: Charles E. Merrill Publishers.

Rogoff, B. (1990) *Apprenticeship in Thinking: cognitive development in social context*. Oxford: Oxford University Press.

Rose, R. (1991) 'A jigsaw approach to group work', *British Journal of Special Education* 18(2), 54–58.

Rose, R. (1998) 'Including pupils: developing a partnership in learning', in Tilstone, C., Florian, L. and Rose, R. (eds) *Promoting Inclusive Practice*. London: Routledge.

Rudduck, J. (1986) 'Curriculum change: management or meaning?', *School Organisation* 6(1), 107–114.

SCAA (School Curriculum and Assessment Authority) (1995) *Planning the Curriculum at Key Stages 1 and 2*. London: SCAA.

SCAA (School Curriculum and Assessment Authority) (1996) *Planning the Curriculum for Pupils with Profound and Multiple Learning Difficulties*. London: SCAA.

Sanderson, H. (1998) 'Person centred planning', in Lacey, P. and Ouvry, C. (eds) *People with Profound and Multiple Learning Disabilities: a collaborative approach to meeting complex needs*. London: David Fulton Publishers.

Schön, D. A. (1991) *The Reflective Practitioner: how professionals think in action*. Aldershot: Ashgate-Arena.

Sebba, J. (1994) *History for All*. London: David Fulton Publishers.

Sebba, J. and Ainscow, M. (1996) 'International developments in inclusive schooling: mapping the issues', *Cambridge Journal of Education* 26(1), 5–17.

Sebba, J., Byers, R. and Rose, R. (1993) *Redefining the Whole Curriculum for Pupils with Learning Difficulties*. London: David Fulton Publishers.

Sebba, J. and Sachdev, D. (1997) *What Works in Inclusive Education?* Ilford, Essex: Barnardos.

Segal, S. (1967) *No Child Is Ineducable: special education: provision and trends*. Oxford: Pergamon Press.

Skrtic, T. M. (1991) 'Students with special educational needs: artefacts of the traditional curriculum', in Ainscow, M. (ed.) *Effective Schools for All*. London: David Fulton Publishers.

Smith, A. (1998) *Accelerated Learning in Practice: brain-based methods for accelerating motivation and achievement*. Stafford: Network Educational Press.

Smith, B. (ed.) (1987) *Interactive Approaches to the Education of Children with Severe Learning Difficulties*. Birmingham: Westhill College.

Smith, B. (1994) 'Handing over control to people with learning difficulties', in Coupe O'Kane, J. and Smith, B. (eds) *Taking Control: enabling people with learning difficulties*. London: David Fulton Publishers.

Solity, J. (1988) ' Systematic assessment and teaching', in Thomas, G. and Feiler, A. (eds) *Planning for Special Needs: a whole-school approach*. Oxford: Basil Blackwell.

Southworth, G. (1998a) *Leading Improving Schools: the work of headteachers and deputy heads.* London: Falmer Press.

Southworth, G. (1998b) 'The learning school: what does it look like?' *Managing Schools Today*, January, 29–30.

Stenhouse, L. (1979) 'What is action-research?' *Norwich C.A.R.E.* Norwich: University of East Anglia.

Sternberg, R. J. (1983) 'Criteria for intellectual skills training', *Educational Researcher* **12**(2), 6–12.

Sternberg, R. J. (1997) *Thinking Styles.* Cambridge: Cambridge University Press.

Stevens, C. (1995) 'News from SCAA', *British Journal of Special Education* **22**(1), 30–31.

Stevens, M. (1971) *The Educational Needs of Severely Subnormal Children.* London: Edward Arnold.

Stoll, L. (1991) 'School effectiveness in action: supporting growth in schools and classrooms', in Ainscow, M. (ed.) *Effective Schools for All.* London: David Fulton Publishers.

Stothard, V. (1998) 'The gradual development of intensive interaction in a school setting', in Hewett, D. and Nind, M. (eds) *Interaction in Action.* London: David Fulton Publishers.

Sugden, D. (1989) 'Special education and the learning process', in Sugden, D. (ed.) *Cognitive Approaches in Special Education.* London: The Falmer Press.

Thomas, G., Walker, D. and Webb, J. (1998) *The Making of the Inclusive School.* London: Routledge.

Tilstone, C. (1991a) 'The class teacher and stress', in Tilstone, C. (ed.) *Teaching Pupils with Severe Learning Difficulties: practical approaches.* London: David Fulton Publishers.

Tilstone, C. (1991b) 'Historical review', in Tilstone, C. (ed.) *Teaching Pupils with Severe Learning Difficulties: practical approaches.* London: David Fulton Publishers.

Tilstone, C. (1991c) 'Pupils' views', in Tilstone, C. (ed.) *Teaching Pupils with Severe Learning Difficulties practical approaches.* London: David Fulton Publishers.

Tilstone, C. and Barry, C. (1998) 'Advocacy and empowerment: what does it mean for pupils and people with PMLD?' in Lacey, P. and Ouvry, C. (eds) *People with Profound and Multiple Learning Disabilities: a collaborative approach to meeting complex needs.* London: David Fulton Publishers.

Tomlinson, P. (1989) 'The teaching of skills: modern cognitive perspectives', in Sugden, D. (ed.) *Cognitive Approaches in Special Education.* London: The Falmer Press.

Tomlinson, S. (1982) *A Sociology of Special Education.* London: Routledge and Kegan Paul.

Turner, J. (1975) *Cognitive Development.* London: Methuen.

UNESCO (1994) *The Salamanca Statement and Framework on Special Needs Education.* Paris: UNESCO.

Vlachou, A. and Barton, L. (1994) 'Inclusive education: teachers and the changing culture of schooling', *British Journal of Special Education* **21**(3), 105–107.

Vygotsky, L. S. (1962) *Thought and Language.* Cambridge, Mass: MIT Press.

Ware, J. (ed.) (1994) *Educating Children with Profound and Multiple Learning Difficulties.* London: David Fulton Publishers.

Weber, K. (1978) *Yes They Can.* Milton Keynes: Open University Press.

Weber, K. (1982) *The Teacher is the Key.* Milton Keynes: Open University Press.

West, M. and Ainscow, M. (1991) *Managing School Development: a practical guide.* London: David Fulton Publishers.

West, N. (1996) 'Subject co-ordinators: they can't make it alone', *Managing Schools Today* **5**(6) March.

White, M. and Cameron, R. J. (1986) *Portage Early Education Programme.* Windsor: NFER-Nelson.

White, O. R. and Haring, N. G. (1980) *Exceptional Teaching.* Columbus, Ohio: Charles E. Merrill Publishing Co.

Wishart, J. (1993) 'Learning the hard way: avoidance strategies in young children with Down's Syndrome'. *Down's Syndrome: Research and Practice* **1**(2), 47–55.

Wood, D. (1998) *How Children Think and Learn,* (2nd edn.). Oxford: Blackwell.

Wood, D. J. , Bruner, J. S. and Ross, G. (1976) 'The role of tutoring in problem solving', *Journal of Child Psychology and Psychiatry* **17**(2), 89–100.

Wright Mills, C. (1959) *The Sociological Imagination.* Oxford: Oxford University Press,

Zarkowska, E. and Clements, J. (1994) *Problem Behaviour and People with Severe Learning Disabilities: the STAR approach,* (2nd edn.). London: Chapman and Hall.

Index